"This book is essential rea[illegible]formers—and seasoned professionals—who n[illegible] want to improve their audition skills, but grow to truly love the process."

- Jeremy Mann (Director of the The Ray Bolger Musical Theater Program, UCLA Department of Theater)

"The entertainment industry is growing and changing all the time. It's so important to have theatre artists like Erik who are sharing their experience so others can succeed and grow."

- Vincent Rodriguez III (Josh Chan on CW's musical TV comedy, Crazy Ex-Girlfriend)

"[Stein] offers a concise, detailed and eminently useful guide to the audition process, guided by the idea that an audition should be crafted with the care of a well-rehearsed one-person show."

- Richard E.T.White (Chair Cornish College of the Arts Theater Department)

"It is an ideal book for students and young professionals who want to audition impressively and build relationships with "the decision makers."

- Roger DeLaurier (Conservatory Director PCPA – Pacific Conservatory Theatre)

"Stein's no-nonsense, practical guide to auditioning has been immensely valuable to the young actors I work with."

- Karin Hendricks (Assistant Professor of Acting and Performance Cal Poly Theatre Department)

"I remain eternally grateful for Erik's guidance. This book is an extension of his ability to encourage talented people to discover their greatness... What a gift!"

- Alisa Taylor (Head of TV / Film / Stage | Bx2 Entertainment)

No Caution

A step-by-step guide to preparing auditions for Universities, Colleges, Conservatories, and Beyond

By
Erik Stein

Copyright © 2019 Erik Stein
All rights reserved. No part of this book may be reproduced or transmitted in any form or by any means, electronical or mechanical, including photocopying, recording, or by any information storage and retrieval system without permission in written form from Erik Stein.

First published in the United States of America in September 2019 by Erik Stein
Library of Congress Control Number: 2019911166

ISBN: 978-0-57854973-6 (Paperback)

Editing by Tamara Stein
Cover Illustration by Carley Herlihy
Formatted by Kathryn Blanche

Printed and bound in the United States of America
First printing September 2019

Distributed by Ingram
www.ingramcontent.com

Printed by Lightning Source

nocautionthebook@gmail.com

DEDICATION

Dedicated to my high school drama teacher Leslie Hinshaw and my after school Community Theatre teacher Sandra Dinse.

TABLE OF CONTENTS

No Caution!

Brittnay Law

INTRODUCTION

You like to do this. You like to get up in front of people and perform. You like doing shows, you like rehearsing, and you love the thrill of opening night. You stand in the wings, excited to go out and share your work and share yourself with the audience. Sure, you're nervous; you don't know how the audience is going to react. You want them to like you, but the unknown of what is about to happen is exhilarating. Some might say that thrilling leap into the unknown is why we do this. So why do so many actors view auditioning as an unpleasant experience?

I like auditions that feel like a one person show. I think the best auditions are the auditions I should have paid to see. When I see a truly great audition I often write, "I should have paid for that" on the actor's resume. I want to feel lucky to have the exclusive ticket to the opening night of your four minute one woman or one man or one person show. I'm not interested in seeing a work in progress. If your only success is that you remembered your lines, that is not enough. I don't want to watch first rehearsal off book. I want to see opening night.

During your training you may have people tell you that you don't want your audition to be "too polished" or "over-rehearsed." What do they mean by that? Let me assure you that I have never said, "Oh, that person is too good. I don't think I can hire them." What worries me is that when someone tells a young actor that they don't want to be too polished or over-rehearsed, the actor often translates that to mean they don't need to prepare as much as they do when getting ready for opening night. Or worse, they think that means they shouldn't make big choices or take risks or take up space or have a big opinion or point of view in an audition, because it might not be what the recruiter or casting director wants.

I can promise you that you will never really know what I want in an audition. You will never know what any of us behind the table wants. There could be three people with three very different opinions behind the table. You will never know exactly what we want to see, and you will drive yourself crazy trying to figure it out.

For example, I like the color yellow. An actor walks into my audition room wearing yellow, I already like them. They have done nothing but walk into the room, and I already have fond feelings for them. On the other hand, I don't like pastels. They are cautious colors, and they piss me off. What is that? Sort of blue?! Be a color, dammit!! Does this mean that the person wearing yellow is getting a callback and the person wearing pastels is not? Of course not, but the person wearing yellow does have an advantage. Is this rational? No. Do you have any control over my crazy? No.

The only thing you have control over is what you want to show me. If you try to cater to what you think I want, if you focus on trying to please me, you will create a cautious audition, and I have no interest in watching a cautious audition.

Jay Binder of Binder Casting in New York says he will sit behind the table in an audition room until he sees the person who walks in and shows him something that is worth a Broadway ticket price on opening night. I have heard teachers tell their students, "Be careful of making a big choice, it may not be what they are looking for." That is awful advice. Cautious actors are not worth Broadway prices.

When I'm recruiting for the Conservatory, I audition approximately 500 actors for 30 spots. Other training programs audition even more actors and accept even fewer. Can you imagine how many actors Jay Binder sees in a week? We are not looking for cautious. Cautious actors suck! I want to see an opening night performance that makes me want to pay you. NO CAUTION!

PART 1

Jerik Fernandez

YOUR FOUR MINUTE SOLO SHOW

PART 1
YOUR FOUR MINUTE SOLO SHOW

What if we don't call it an audition anymore? What if we call it your show? Someone asks you what you're doing this weekend, you say, "I'm gonna go do my show for Carnegie Mellon." You're flying to Chicago to attend the Unifieds, you say, "I'm doing my show for a sold out house in Chicago." In February, you're traveling to meet several different schools in several different cities, you say, "I'm taking my show on tour." You like to do shows. You take time, and you put in the effort to rehearse your show.

I once had a student call me six days before their audition for UCLA and ask me for help getting ready for their audition. They hadn't even selected their monologues and songs yet. I had a student call me at 9:00 a.m. asking for a Shakespeare monologue for their 1:00 p.m. USC audition. Can you imagine an opening night with only 6 days of rehearsal? How would you feel if you got a new song four hours before curtain on opening night?

Actors will put so much effort into getting a show ready, yet they often treat auditions like an afterthought. That makes no sense. You don't get to do the show if your audition is crap, and you don't get to come to my school if you don't care enough to prepare like you are preparing for opening night.

> **Note:** This book is designed to help students prepare for university, college, and conservatory auditions. However, these are professional techniques. The philosophy and the steps we are about to explore will work for actors who are new to this as well as for actors who have trained and are part of the professional world.

So how do we prepare?

I want you to start thinking like a decision maker. I call recruiters, directors, choreographers, musical directors, casting directors... decision makers. These are the people sitting behind the table in the audition room. Instead of trying to figure out what the decision maker wants to see, think about what you would want to see if you were the decision maker.

For example, let's say you're auditioning for the role of Sophie in *Mamma Mia*. What if instead of asking the director and musical director what song you should sing for the audition, you ask yourself what you would want to see if you were casting the role of Sophie. You can't control what I want to see, but you can control what you want to show me. If you focus on what you think I want to see, you will create a cautious audition.

Let's create the four minute one man or one woman or one person show you would want to see if you were the decision maker sitting behind the table.

> **Note:** Actors often create one person shows. They are commonly referred to as one man shows or one woman shows. I remember the first time I saw Audra McDonald's one woman show. It changed my life. For the purpose of this book, I'm going to use the term "Solo Show". As our society evolves, we are finding that the terms one man show and one woman show do not include everyone. This book, the theatre... the world is for everyone, so from here on out we will call it your four minute solo show.

1. GET YOUR MATERIAL EARLY

Schools can have different requirements. Many schools will want one contemporary monologue, one Shakespeare monologue, and a portion of one song. Some schools will want two songs and one monologue; some may ask for two Shakespeare pieces and no song. There are several different combinations.

Make sure you are very aware of how long they want each piece to be. Some schools will say each monologue should be no longer than two minutes, some ask for no longer than 90 seconds, and a few even ask for no longer than 60 seconds. ***Do not go over time.***

The first thing you need to do is make sure you fully understand what material each school wants to see. I recommend you have a binder or a spreadsheet that dedicates a section to each school that interests you. On the first page of each section, list the application and audition requirements for that school. For our purposes, I am going to assume that you need one contemporary monologue, one Shakespeare monologue, and a portion of one song. Each monologue should not be any longer than 90 seconds, and your song should be no longer than 32 bars. This will be your four-minute solo show.

We will talk more about how to find strong material later. For now, let me just say: Read plays. See plays. Listen to musicals. Watch musicals. Talk to your friends. Steal from those who have gone before you. Find your material early so you can fall in love with the pieces you choose. You want material that fits you and excites you, so that when you are waiting in the hall you are excited to show the decision makers the pieces you've picked.

Can you imagine standing in the wings on the opening night of *The Crucible* having had the script for just a few days?

Can you imagine standing in the wings on opening night, and you don't really like the play you are about to perform?

2. FIND A DIRECTOR

Allison F. Rich and Carley Herlihy.

Chloe Babbes and Brad Carroll

You need someone you trust to guide you. You need that outside eye to give you feedback. It could be your teacher, a local theatre professional, a graduate, anyone you think has the experience to help you create your four-minute solo show.

There are great online coaches. I recommend Faith Prince and Natasha Hause at Minimoon Studios. www.minimoon.com

I also like Musical Theatre College Auditions. www.mtcollegeauditions.com

I also do online coaching. You can reach me at NoCautionTheBook@gmail.com.

Can you imagine trying to get to opening night of *Peter and the Starcatcher* without a director? I dare say it would be a mess.

3. REHEARSE, REHEARSE, REHEARSE...

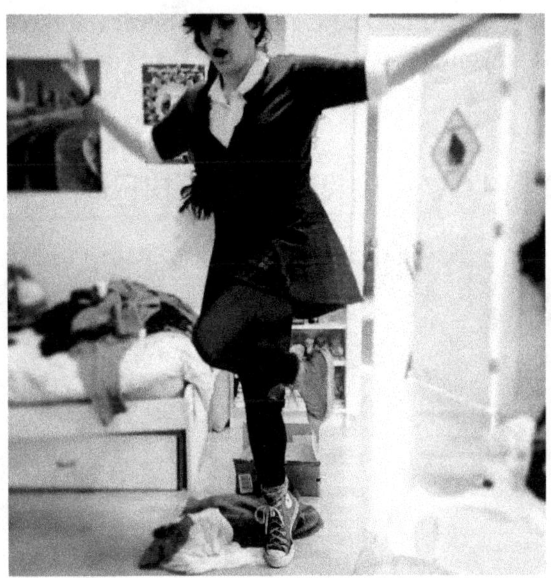

Maya Sherer

Create a rehearsal schedule. I suggest you plan at least four weeks to get ready. Meet with your director or coach at least once a week. Spend the first week working on one monologue, spend the second week working on your second monologue, and spend the third week working on your song. That leaves the fourth week for dress rehearsals and previews. In between your coaching sessions, do each of your pieces full out (standing and out loud) at least twice a day. This is all very doable. You just have to make a plan and stick to it.

You may think you are a great improv actor. Do not try to improvise your audition. You are not that good. Meryl Streep rehearses, Denzel Washington rehearses... the greats rehearse. Be great.

Some might say, "You don't want to rehearse too much. You don't want to be too polished." I assume that to be "too polished" could mean mechanical, unmotivated, unconnected, unintentional, presentational, or undirectable, and, sure, I don't want to see any of that on opening night, but I don't think an unmotivated, presentational, undirectable performance is the result of over-rehearsing. I just think that's bad acting.

On opening night, your cast mates trust that you have put the time in to be ready for the show. You would never want to let them down. Don't let yourself down. Do the work, so you can trust yourself.

4. HAVE DRESS REHEARSALS

Maya Sherer

Clothes can really change how you move. Characters are often built from the shoes up. Life is different when you are wearing heels instead of flip flops. You move differently in dress shoes than you do in Converse. A nice summer dress feels very different than yoga pants. You are a different person when you wear a tie instead of a hoodie. You need to do dress rehearsals.

I recommend you ***always*** rehearse in the shoes you plan to wear, and I think you must do one or two rehearsals in your audition outfit with your hair styled while (if you plan to wear make-up) wearing make-up. How many times have you felt like your performance got better once you had the costume on? Well, put on your costume and rehearse. We will talk later in the book about how to put together your audition outfit, but for now, let's just agree that you are going to have a few dress rehearsal before opening night.

Imagine you are playing Elle Woods in *Legally Blonde*. How would you feel on opening night if you had never rehearsed while wearing heels? You step out on stage to sing "Omigod You Guys" wearing three-inch heels for the first time. I fear that is a disaster waiting to happen.

5. HAVE A PREVIEW PERFORMANCE

Johnny Davison, Antwon Mason, Meami Maszewski, Iven Webster, Jerik Fernandez, Ella Ruth Francis, Bianca Norwood, Myles Romo

Most professional theatre companies have what are called "Previews" before opening night. In the professional theatre, a preview is a performance that allows audience members to see the show before the critics are allowed to see it. This gives the actors, the director, the designers, and all involved the opportunity to see how the show plays and how the audience is reacting before critics see the show.

Theatres continue to rehearse during preview performances, and they make adjustments from what they learn. At PCPA, we do a preview performance for members of the Conservatory on Wednesday, then preview performances for friendly audiences on Thursday and Friday. We continue to rehearse in the afternoons on those days, and then we open on Saturday night.

I recommend you do a couple of preview performances. If you can stand in front of your drama class and do your four-minute solo show in the clothes and shoes you plan to wear, you can stand in front of me. Your classmates have known you since you were five. They know all your tricks and habits. They love you, but you can't sneak anything by them. If you can stand in your living room and do your solo show for your family, then trust me, you can do it for me.

How many times have you wished you knew on opening night what you know on closing? Do some preview performances, so you will have all the confidence you need on opening night.

Respect yourself enough to do the work to be ready. There will always be an element of the unknown during an audition, just like there are unknowns on opening night, but if we prepare and do the work, the unknown can be thrilling rather than terrifying.

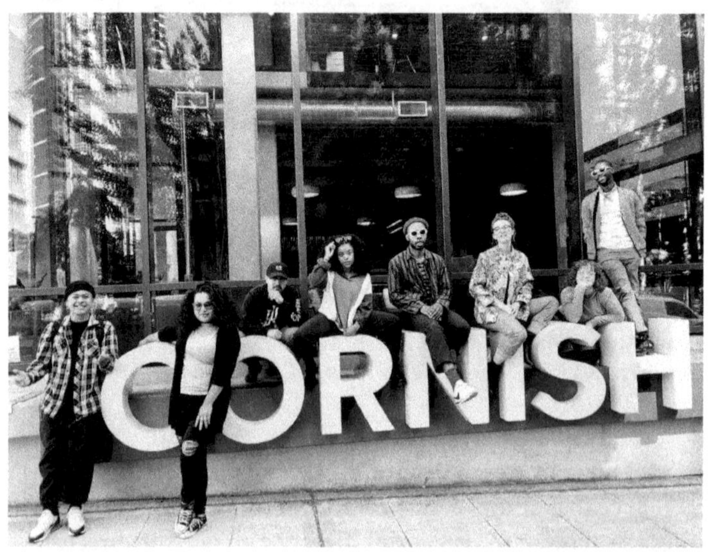

Jerik Fernandez, Alyssa Anderson, Myles Romo, Natalia Womack, Brandon Jones Mooney, Quincy Van Steenberge, Jackie Thompson, Vintre Scott

PART 2

Brittany Law

STEP BY STEP

Vocal #1 (1 of 5)
15
Under impression
anything
"Tallest"?

PART TWO: STEP BY STEP

The title of this book promises you a step-by-step guide to prepare your audition. Well, first, let's change the word audition to show, and let's spend some time focusing on what you do once you walk into the audition room. The last section got you prepared for your opening night. This next section is a checklist you can think about while you are waiting in the hall about to share your opening night performance.

During the following pages, please know that absolutely everything I say about a monologue applies to a song. Many young actors think that they share their monologues to show me they can act and share their songs to show me they can sing. Let go of that way of thinking. Your song is just another way to show me what an amazing actor you are.

Whitney Bacon and Madison Davis

When you sing, you must be more than just a vessel for sound. Assume that everyone who auditions for me can sing. You have to be more. Use your contemporary monologue to show me what an amazing contemporary actor you are, use your Shakespeare piece to show me what an amazing classical actor you are, and use your song to show me what an amazing musical theatre actor you are. You are an actor with many marketable skills.

Skye Privat

STEP 1: CONNECT

Poised is poisonous. I want to meet the authentic you. Many young actors think they need to be "professional" when they walk into the room. However, it seems students often think that "professional" means polite with no personality—a robot who only responds with one word answers and only when spoken to.

I often hear young actors tell me they "don't want to waste my time." I am looking for the three P's: Passion, Preparation, and Potential. If you have potential, if you are prepared, and if you are passionate, you are not wasting my time.

I like actors who are confident without being cocky. Confidence is attractive, cocky is not. Confident people are prepared and they let me see their passion. Cocky people hide their passion.

Stephen Book says in his truly interesting book, *An Actor Takes a*

Meeting, that actors often view auditions like a victim: as if you have been summoned to this place to appear in front of this person or these people of power—almost like you've been called to the principal's office to be punished. Stephen suggests that you let go of being a victim and instead view the audition as an event in which you are the host.

What if you walk into the room as if you are the host of this event? You want to make sure that your guests are comfortable, have what they need, and are enjoying themselves. Your guests are either people you care about or people you would like to get to know. You are in the room as equals. You both have something you need, and you both have something to give.

If you truly and authentically want to share yourself, your talent, and your passion with me, if you truly want to put me at ease, then I will see a confident young actor who does not even know the meaning of the word cocky.

Natalia Womack

So, let's be honest. Some of this is easier said than done. How does one bring one's authentic self into the room? Who am I? What is my authentic self? Hard questions to answer.

As actors, we learn that you can't play a quality. You don't go into a scene and play "I am happy." Happy is a quality. Instead, you might play that you want to celebrate with your friend. The result may be that you are happy, but you are focused on celebrating with your friend. To celebrate with your friend is your intention. Happiness is the result.

I believe that everything in life is better with an intention. If you have an intention when you walk into the room, that means you have something to do when you walk into the room. You are not trying to be something, you are just doing. If your intention involves me, the guy sitting behind the desk, then I get to be part of what you are doing. My wonderful friend and colleague Karin Hendricks refers to this as creating a horizontal experience. If your intention involves me, then we are having a horizontal experience. If your intention involves only you, then you are having a vertical experience. I am more likely to experience your authentic self during a horizontal experience.

> **Note:** Your intention should be a verb. Verbs allow you to do; adjectives are results. For example, instead of playing that you are *confused*, let your character have the intention to *question*. By questioning your surroundings, the result could be that you are perceived as confused.
>
> Ado Annie in *Oklahoma* does not try to play dumb; neither should the actor who plays her. Ado Annie is questioning. She is trying to find the answers in the eyes of her best friend. It's as if she is trying to put together a difficult puzzle. We get to watch Ado Annie horizontally do something, and because of what she is doing, we may perceive her as not quite the brightest bulb on the tree.

So, if you are the host of this event, what is a good horizontal intention you can play when you walk into the room? I like the simple intention: to connect. You are the host of this event, I am your guest, and your intention is to connect with me. You are standing in the hall, you are waiting to go in, and you think to yourself, "I am the host of this event. I want to put the person behind the table at ease, and I am going to do that by trying to connect."

What are some ways we can "connect" with the person behind the table? I recommend you do not try to initiate a handshake. Decision makers meet a lot of people. Recruitment season often happens during flu season. Some people may not want to shake a lot of hands. If the decision maker behind the table initiates the handshake, then yes, please shake their hand, but let your guest be the person to put their hand out first.

One way to connect when you enter the room is by speaking. Smile as you walk through the door and maybe say "Hi," or "Good morning," or "Good to see you," or "Thanks for seeing me." I recommend you avoid asking questions right when you walk in the room. The person behind the table may still be writing notes about the person before you. You don't want to put them in a position where they have to respond. If you say, "How are you?" as you walk in the room, and they don't respond, you just created an awkward situation. If the person behind the table is obviously not ready to connect with you, maybe you try to connect with the person behind the piano instead. You're the host of the party. Read the energy of the room, so you can avoid awkward situations.

I think the best way to try to connect is to try to make eye contact. Try to actually have your eyes look into my eyes.

Vintre Scott

Here's a secret. The best horizontal intentions are ones at which you can fail. Say you walk in the room and want to connect with me by making eye contact, and I am not looking at you. That's ok. It doesn't change the fact that you want to connect with me. You get to keep looking for ways to do it. If you can't connect with me right when you walk in, maybe you can shift and connect with the piano player. If you succeed with the piano player, start looking for opportunities to connect with me. You introduce yourself, I look up, we look into each other's eyes - boom! Success! We just connected. You continue to put me at ease by introducing your pieces and your song.

Rehearse how you are going to talk to the piano player. It's part of your show, and it is a good way for the person behind the table to see how you authentically deal with people.

When you talk to the piano player you should be kind, clear, and efficient. There is no need to rush, yet please be efficient. I recommend you smile, say hello, and thank them for playing for you. Only shake their hand if they initiate it. As you place the music on the piano, let them know the title of your piece. Show them where you want them to start playing and where you want them to stop. Let them know what your tempo is by singing the first few bars of the song. Don't snap the tempo at them, don't thump it out on the piano, just sing a few bars until they indicate that they got it. Point out any surprises in the song. Does it speed up somewhere? Does it ritard? Are you taking the second ending? Is there a fermata?

Rehearse your song with a piano player before your audition.

Can you imagine going to opening night having only ever sung your song with the Broadway cast recording?

Can you imagine standing on stage on opening night having never heard the exact intro to your song?

Make sure your music is clearly marked. Have an arrow that says "start here". Make sure it is pointing at where you want them to start playing, not where you plan to start singing. Have an arrow that shows them where they should stop playing, and highlight any surprises. Have a skilled accompanist help you mark your music, so the piano player in the room can help you succeed during your four-minute solo show.

Rehearse how you are going to introduce yourself and your pieces. Some people call it your "slate." I want you to know what you want to say, but please, don't be a robot. Alisa Taylor is a manager with Bx2 Entertainment, a PCPA graduate, and a wonderful friend, and she says it so well: "When you introduce yourself, be a person." ***Remember, poised is poisonous. Connect with me. Put me at ease.***

That will allow me to see who you really are. The information I need is your name, the title of the play for each monologue, and the title of the song you plan to sing. Create the intro or slate that works for *you.* Some people also tell me the name of the character from the play and what musical the song is from, but it is your show. Be efficient, be clear, and let me see you. Breathe and be alive in the moment. Read the energy of the room. Connect with me and see if there is an instant when we actually really see each other.

I'm trying to figure out if I want to spend two years with you. Most schools are looking to see if they want to spend four years with you. I've got your monologues and your song to assess your potential. I've only got the moment you walk in the room, your time at the piano, your introduction, and your exit to figure out who you are. Don't hide behind being polite. Don't cover with a cocky attitude. Connect with me, and let me see your passion.

Bianca Norwood and Quincy Van Steenberge

Isaac Capp and Robert Kiner

STEP 2: WHO ARE YOU TALKING TO?

Now that you've connected with me and introduced your pieces, it is time to transition to your first piece. Unless the decision maker behind the table or the application instructions say otherwise, you can go in any order you would like. I recommend you sing last, because that gives the accompanist time to look over your music while you are doing your monologues, but you can sing first if that works better for you. It's your show.

Some people say you should start with your strongest piece, some say you should end with your strongest. I say you should wow me at the beginning and leave me with something wonderful. If you are new to Shakespeare or you are not yet comfortable as a singer, do that in the middle. Decision makers tend to make up their minds quickly. Hook me right away with the opening scene of your solo show and leave me wanting more.

Be efficient as you transition from your intro to your first piece. You do not need to drop your head and take time to get centered. You don't need to turn your back and shake out the nerves. You wouldn't do that in front of the audience on opening night. Do that stuff off-stage and walk into the room ready. The transitions from your intro to your first piece and between your pieces are part of your show. They should be part of your rehearsal process.

I will offer more detailed advice on how to transition from piece to piece later in the book when I talk you through your solo show from beginning to end.

As you work on your monologues and songs, be sure you know whom you are talking to and whom you are singing to. This is very important. Know your target.

I like the word "target". You want your monologues and your songs to be horizontal experiences. You must be targeting someone, and that person needs to be the reason you are talking or singing. That person needs to be the reason these specific words are necessary. I need to believe that if I took that person away, you would have no reason to speak or sing.

WHO?

Natalia Womack and Carley Herlihy

Who are you talking to? Who are you targeting? Get super specific. Is it your mom? Your boyfriend? Your best friend? A homeless person? A cop? Someone who kidnapped you? Someone you kidnapped? There are so many options, but whoever it is, it must be someone who can be affected by you- someone who can be changed by you.

I recommend that you do not choose a therapist as your target. Their job is to just listen and not be affected. Don't choose God. You have no idea if you are affecting God, and don't talk on the phone. You and the person you are trying to affect need to be in the same room.

I think it is best to target just one person. It is easier to affect one person than a crowd. If you must talk to more than one person, I suggest you talk to no more than three. You can keep track of whether or not you are affecting three people.

Do not talk to yourself. That creates a vertical experience, and I want to watch a horizontal experience. I want to watch you fight to change your scene partner or your "other". I want to watch you fight to win. Acting is doing. I want to watch you do something. If you are talking to yourself, then it is likely you are just being.

I understand that in many plays people stand on stage and talk to themselves. Shakespeare writes a lot of soliloquies. There are arguments to be made about who they are actually talking to, but for our purposes, remember you are crafting a four-minute solo show. You have a very brief time to show me what you can do. Don't waste time *being* by talking to yourself. Show me what an amazing actor you are by *doing*. Talk to someone. Target someone. Fight to win.

Often, you can figure out who you are talking to by looking at the circumstances of the play from which you found your monologue. That's great, but sometimes the circumstances work for a two hour play but not for your four-minute solo show. You can reimagine the piece slightly to make it work for your show. For example, let's pretend you want to sing part of "Maria" from *West Side Story*. In the musical, Tony is walking the streets singing by himself. In your show, what if he is singing to his grandmother? Let's say she has been the most important thing in his life. She raised him. You can play that you want to make your grandmother smile, you want her to meet Maria, you want her to stay alive so she can come to your wedding, you want her blessing... There are a lot of things you can play that involve your grandmother. The decision maker behind the table doesn't need to know that you've changed the circumstances for your show. I don't need to know you are singing to your grandmother. I just want to watch you have a horizontal experience where you try to change someone.

You could also play that Tony is searching for an ally. He stands in the middle of the street, and he sings to anyone who will listen. You must have specific targets. Generality is the death of good art. Tony could target a homeless person on the street, a cop walking by, a lady leaning out her window.... He's trying to get them on his side, on his team. He tries to win allies who will support him as he fights to win Maria's love.

WHERE?

Let's get even more specific. Where is the person you are talking to? Are they close or are they far away? Is this a public moment or a private moment? Are they standing or sitting? Are you in the kitchen or outside? Really know where your other is. Once that is clear, you don't have to stare at them the whole time. That makes you look like a crazy stalker. When we talk to someone, we don't stare at them the whole time. Establish where your other is and then live in the space. You always know where your other is, but you don't have to stand in one spot the whole time. Carve your space. When do you look away from your scene partner? When do you walk away? The decision maker behind the table doesn't need to know exactly where you are, but you do. I want to feel like I am watching a show, not a recitation.

I recommend you do not talk to an empty chair. Sometimes young actors will put a chair in the space and talk to it like there is someone sitting in it. I don't like that. I end up staring at the empty chair instead of watching you. You don't need it. The empty chair just advertises that no one is actually there. You're a good actor. Trust that you can convince me that you are talking to someone without putting an empty chair in your show.

> **Note:** Do not use the person behind the table as your scene partner. When connecting with the person behind the table during your intro, you make eye contact. You look into my eyes. However, after you transition to your pieces, do not play directly to my eyes. Find a target that allows me to see your face well, but do not do your piece directly to me behind the table. I do not want to be your scene partner. I want to be your audience. I want to watch your show, I do not want to be in it. On rare occasions, the person behind the table might ask you to do your pieces or one of your pieces directly to her or him. If the person asks you to, then, of course, do it, but only

if they request it.

WHAT?

Let's go even deeper. What is your other doing? Are they leaving the room, and you are trying to get them to stay? Are they sitting down, and you are trying to get them to stand? Are they standing, and you are trying to get them to sit? Are they playing video games, and you are trying to get them to put the controller down? Are they doing the dishes, and you are trying to get them to look at you? Are they pointing a gun at you, and you are trying to get them to put the gun down? Are they pointing a gun at themselves, and you are trying to get them to put the gun down? There are endless possibilities, and your other must be doing something.

If your other is just standing there politely listening to you, that is not enough. Your job is to fight to change that person. You are fighting to win.

I think the best question to ask is, "What do I want to make that person do right now?" They are leaving, and I am trying to get them to stay. Their back is to me, and I am trying to get them to turn around.

I think a great journey of a monologue or song could be: At first my other is leaving, and I fight to make them stay. I win, they stay. Now their back is to me, and I fight to make them turn around. I win, they turn around. Now I fight to make my other walk towards me. Do I win? I don't know. It could change every time I do the piece.

I recommend you use your words to make your other do something right now. Your scene partner is someone I can't see. I don't need a lot of blocking or pantomime. You should feel free to move, but instead of pretending to grab your scene partner, stop them with your words.

Again, you can figure out what your other is doing by looking at the circumstances of the play from which you found your monologue. That's great, but often the circumstances work for a two hour play, but not for your four minute solo show. You can reimagine the piece slightly to make it work for your show. For example, let's pretend you are doing Christopher Durang's tuna fish monologue from *Laughing Wild*—the one where you talk about someone hitting you on the head in the grocery store. In the play the character is talking to the audience, but in your show let's say you are talking to a burglar who you caught breaking into your house. You've tied him to a chair. What is he doing? He is trying to get free. He's making a lot of noise. You've had a really bad day. You're not sure what to do with him, but you know you need to quiet him. You need him to be still, so you can think. You tell him about your tuna fish day to scare him or to shut him up or to knock him off balance. The person behind the table doesn't need to know that you've changed the circumstances for your show. I don't need to know you have a burglar tied up in your kitchen; I just want to watch you have a horizontal experience where I get to watch you use your words to try to make someone do something right now—where I get to watch you fight to win.

Chloe Babbes and Cheyenne Omani

So, who are you talking to, where are they, and what are they doing? I suggest you rehearse your pieces by turning them into scenes. Ask one of your fellow actors to be your scene partner. Do your monologues to them. Sing your song to your friend. Don't let them just stand there and politely listen to you. Turn it into the scene you have imagined. Tell your friend to start to leave and stop only if your words and intention stop them. See if you can make them turn around with your words. Try to make them walk towards you with your words. Don't be shy about asking a fellow actor to help you. You would help your friend, so feel sure they would help you. Take what you learn by actually having a scene partner and use it on the opening night of your solo show.

Maya Sherer

STEP 3: MOMENT BEFORE

Now that you are very clear about who you are talking to, where they are, and what they are doing, you must ask yourself, "What did that person do that affects me and makes me have to speak?" You must have a reason to speak. The words must be necessary. You must have a reason to sing. Something must happen that is so life altering that mere words are not enough; you must sing.

What your other does to make you have to speak or sing is called your "moment before"—and I want to see it. When I see a young actor with a brief moment before, I immediately assume that this person is more advanced.

Hear me when I say that I am not looking for an elaborate pantomime before you start to speak. I am hoping for something that is one to two seconds long—seriously, no longer than two seconds. A desperate inhale, questioning eyes, the desire to step forward, or a glance to where someone may be at any moment is enough. It needs to be short, yet it should also be obvious. ***I want a very short, obvi-***

ous moment before.

The moment before is necessary, because you must have something that triggers your need to fight to win. Your show is short. We don't have time for a lot of exposition. We are starting these pieces at moments of life-altering need. Without a moment before, you may spend the first 15 seconds of your 90 second piece warming up. There's a good chance I've already formed an opinion about you in the first 15 seconds. The moment before triggers your need to speak, your need to sing.

Here is a possible scenario for a contemporary monologue: Paul is recently married. He innocently takes notice of a beautiful woman at the counter while he is waiting in line with his new wife for a cup of coffee. His wife sees him take notice of the beautiful woman. Paul sees her see him taking notice. His wife is upset; she rolls her eyes and turns to leave. Paul must use his words to keep his wife in the coffee shop. If she leaves, Paul will feel awful.

Now, I don't need to see all of that. I just need to see the moment that triggers Paul's need to speak. I don't need to know anything about the other woman during the moment before; I don't even need to know he is married. I just need to see a moment of desperation as he frantically tries to find the words to keep his wife in the coffee shop. I suggest the moment before be the moment Paul sees his wife roll her eyes. It takes less than two seconds, but it is an important two seconds.

I once had a student use the rejection of a proposal of marriage as his moment before his song. Unfortunately, he decided his moment before needed to be to take out the ring, kneel, open the box, hold it out to her, feel her rejection, stand, watch her turn away, then sing. That is too much.

He kept the scenario, but now he starts from the moment she turns away. He has all of the fuel of what happened, but the moment before that I see is his heartbreak as she turns away from him.

Remember, I don't need to know exactly what you are doing. I just need to know that you are doing something. Trust that it will become clearer as the piece proceeds. I just need to be drawn in by your moment before, and, more importantly, you need to be affected by your moment before.

Simply put, I want to see the scene start before you start to speak, and you need a trigger to fuel your need to speak.

Your moment before needs to be something you can say in very few words. It is much easier to be affected by, “She rolls her eyes,” than it is, “We are recently married, and my wife is very insecure about her looks. Whenever we go out in public she worries that I am looking at other women. I love my wife. I think she is the most beautiful person ever. I would never cheat on her. I just happened to notice a woman standing in line. It was harmless. My wife totally overreacted and started to leave....” All of this information might be useful back story, but it is too much for a moment before. You can’t play a paragraph in an instant. Find the exact moment that triggers you.

See how few words you can use to describe your moment before. “They pull out knives and start to walk towards me.” “She drops the ring.” “He turns away.” “He smiles.” “She spits on me.” “Her eyes fill with tears.” “He slapped me.” “He raises the gun to his head.” “She says yes.” There is great power in simplicity.

I know I’ve said this before, but you can figure out what your moment before is by looking at the circumstances of the play or musical from which you found your monologue or song. However, sometimes the circumstances work for a two hour play, but not for your four minute solo show. You can reimagine the piece slightly to make it work for your show. For example, let’s pretend you are doing Madge’s monologue to Hal at the dance from William Inge’s *Picnic*. In the play Hal has just been verbally assaulted by a local school teacher. Hal is off by himself. Madge approaches him.

This works well in the play, but for the monologue alone we need a trigger to raises the stakes—to make these words necessary right now. We need something tailored specifically for the needs of your show. What if the moment before is, “He grabs a bottle of scotch and starts to take off the cap.” The person behind the table doesn’t need to know that you’ve changed the circumstances for your show. I don’t need to know that Hal is about to take a drink. I just want to watch you have a horizontal experience where you try to affect someone. Where I get to watch you fight to win.

I recommend that you inhale in your moment before. Many young actors will start with a brief, specific, and useful moment before, and right before they speak, they exhale. Honestly, that kind of kills the moment. When you exhale before you speak, you are putting your intention on the exhale instead of on the words.

Remember, your moment before is fueling your need to speak. When Hal puts that bottle of scotch to his lips, inhale and then speak to stop him. When your other points a gun at you, inhale that terror and then speak to save your life. When Curly sees the sun rising over a field of Oklahoma corn, he doesn't exhale and then sing the word, "Oh". He inhales the overwhelming beauty, and he sings, "Oh, what a beautiful morning." Shakespeare doesn't want you to exhale and then say, "Oh, for a muse of fire...." He wants you to inhale your moment before and then change all who are listening with the word "Oh".

Again, it can be very helpful to find a scene partner and rehearse your monologues and songs as if they are scenes. Let your friend in on the specifics of your moment before. Rehearse several times actually vocalizing and physicalizing your moment before as part of your scene.

Let's use the Christopher Durang tuna fish monologue as an example. You could have your scene partner pretend to be tied to a chair. Have them struggle, swear at you, and demand to be set free. Inhale what they are doing, and then use the words to see if you can silence them before the cops come. Or how about the monologue from *Picnic*? Give your scene partner a bottle and have them open it. Inhale that moment and see if you can keep him from taking that first drink using only your words.

After you have rehearsed your moment before with a scene partner, work on doing it alone, without someone actually there acting it out. Streamline your moment before. Find its essence. Remember, no more than two seconds. Any longer and it's awkward and you look like an amateur. If it's only half a second, that's ok. I will see it if it is specific and useful.

Your moment before is for you, it is not for me. However, if I can see that you really have a reason to speak, that you really have a reason to sing, I will see an advanced young actor who is ready for more.

Maya Sherer

STEP 4: DISCOVERY

Often when I am watching an audition I find myself drawn in at first, but then I lose interest. The actor has a clear other whom they are fighting to change right now, he or she had a brief yet obvious moment before that triggered a clear need to speak, yet two thirds of the way through the piece I lose interest. Why?

My mentor, colleague, and wonderful friend Roger DeLaurier says he wants to see actors do more than just report information. In auditions, it often seems as if the character has already figured out what they want to say, and they just come out and say it. They just report the information. They may report it passionately, they may report it in a funny way, but when they started the piece, they already knew they were going to win. If you already know the end of the play, why go on the journey?

Often, when watching auditions, I feel like the actor put a puzzle together offstage in the wings and then walked out on stage and showed me a completed picture. I want to watch you put the puzzle together in front of me. I want to a see a character who is struggling to hold all of the pieces. I want to watch the character try to make the pieces fit together, and then I want to watch the character discover the picture in front of me.

Willow Orthwein

Discovery is the secret. Discovery is what sets the pros apart from the amateurs. Something unexpected must happen to your character. What surprises you? Where does the light bulb turn on? As Oprah would say, "Where is your "Aha" moment?" Where is the discovery?

As you work on your pieces, ask yourself, "What do I know at the end of the piece that I didn't know at the beginning, and where do I discover it?" Once you answer that question, you can identify where the discovery happens.

Sometimes young actors will tell me that they make a discovery on the last line of their piece, and that is fine. However, I need you to also find discovery early enough in the piece that it allows you to change how you are dealing with your other. Often what makes me lose interest is the actor is just playing the same tactic for the whole piece.

A tactic is the thing you do to try to change your other. For example, what if you see someone in a chair and you want to make that person stand. You might start by trying to intimidate them and bully them. You yell at them, "Get out of the chair!" But what if you discover that they can't stand? They broke their hip and can't get out of the chair. Because of this discovery, you are going to need to change how you deal with the person. It makes no since to continue bullying them yelling, "Get out of the chair!" You need to try something different. Maybe you change your tactic to assist or lift the person out of the chair. That could be an interesting journey. I see you bullying a person in a chair, yelling, "Get out of the chair!", you make a discovery that the person can't stand, and so you shift to assisting that person in the chair. You offer a caring hand and say, "Let me help you out of the chair." That's a show I'd like to watch.

Discovery allows you to change your tactic.

Here's a more detailed scenario: The given circumstances may be that you are breaking up with your boyfriend, because he cheated on you. Your intention may be to make him leave the room. A tactic you might use to make him leave the room is to shame him. That's a good situation with a clear and active intention and tactic, but if all you do is shame him for the whole monologue, I am going to lose interest. You need to make a discovery.

What if we try the same scenario, but half way through your piece you discover that you can't live without him? Because of this discovery, you now want to keep him in the room, and you try a new tactic. Maybe you plead with him. That could be an interesting journey. Your moment before is your boyfriend telling you he loves another woman. You want to make him leave the room. You use your words to shame him, but as he leaves, you discover you can't live without him. You are now desperate for him to stay. You use your words to plead with him. Do you win? Do you get what you want? That doesn't matter. What matters is I got to watch you fight to change your other. I got to watch you deal with something unexpected, and I got to watch you try to change your other in a new way.

That is the secret. ***Something unexpected must happen, so I can watch you deal with the unexpected.***

Julliard graduate, PCPA alumn, and wonderful friend Bianca Norwood taught me that a monologue, a song, a scene, a play is like a calm pool of water. At first the water is still. We don't know what is just beneath the surface. At some point someone drops a pebble in the pond and the smooth surface is disrupted. The water is now rough, there are waves, what was underneath is churning to the top, and you must now figure out how to calm the water.

(Above) Bianca Norwood
(Right) Bianca Norwood's acceptance letter from Juilliard

The Juilliard School

March 15, 2017

Juilliard

Dear Bianca,

Congratulations! It gives me tremendous pleasure to inform you that the Juilliard Drama faculty and the Committee on Admissions have granted you admission to the Bachelor of Fine Arts program at The Juilliard School for the 2017-18 academic year. Enrollment at Juilliard is an opportunity to join a community of accomplished performing artists from around the world in an exciting and challenging education. We would like to extend to you every encouragement to join us in the fall!

When you are working on your monologues and your songs, ask yourself, "Where does the pebble drop?" and "What do I need to do to navigate these newly rough waters?"

Your piece can have more than one discovery—I'd love to see multiple discoveries—but you must have at least one. If your character doesn't discover anything, then they are just reporting information, and I want to watch you do more than just report information.

Discovery can also be enhanced by exploring whether this is a public moment between you and your other or a private moment. Do you want the room to hear what you are saying to your other, or is this just between you and him? Maybe it changes with discovery.

Using our previous example, what if your boyfriend tells you he is in love with another woman, and you start trying to make him leave the room by publicly shaming him. You want everybody in the room to witness what you are doing to him, but you see something in his eyes that makes you discover that you can't live without him. You now want him to stay and you privately plead with him. You no longer want to share this with the room. It is a private horizontal moment between you and your boyfriend. Do you win? I don't know; it could change every time you do the piece, but I saw a layered and thrilling journey. I saw a skilled actor who knows how to play multiple tactics.

Remind yourself when you are working on your pieces that your characters don't know they are going to win. There can be no discovery if you already know—no reason to fight if you already know you're going to win.

This is called playing the end of the scene. We want to avoid this. Instead, start the scene with your intention, encounter obstacles, make discoveries, and change your tactics. If you already know the end of the scene, there are no obstacles, there is no discovery, and there is no need to change your tactics. That's boring. Omniscient or all-knowing characters are boring. I want to watch flawed characters struggle to change their other right now. I want to see something unexpected happen, and I want to watch you deal with the unexpected.

It can be hard to find discovery in a narrative monologue. A narrative monologue is a monologue that talks about something that already happened. It's a story monologue. Often young actors will choose a monologue that tells me a story about something that already happened. They may tell it passionately, they may tell it in a funny way, but there is no discovery, because the story already happened. They are just reporting something that occurred in the past. We will talk more about finding good material later in the book, but remember it is very hard to find discovery in a narrative monologue.

Songs often hand the discovery to you. I once had the fortune of observing a workshop led by Jason Robert Brown; he laid the journey of a song out so beautifully. He told us that you can often find the reason for the song in the last line of the bridge. When you are working on a song, pay special attention to the bridge. The music often changes during the bridge, because discovery is often made in the bridge. Often there is a key change right after the bridge, because a big discovery was made that was so life altering a new key was warranted.

I love singing in an audition, because the song hands you everything you need. You can have your moment before during the intro, you can use your first tactic to change your other during the first verse, you can have life altering discovery during the bridge, and then have a new tactic as you fight to win in the final verse.

> **Note:** Often auditions will ask for only 32 bars of a song. 32 bars is often the bridge to the end of the song. When crafting your 32 bars, I recommend you try to include the bridge. The bridge allows you to have life altering discovery and a reason to sing the final verse.

I like that phrase, "Life-altering discovery." I like watching pieces that are life changing. I want to believe that the character will never be the same because of the life-altering discovery I just witnessed.

I also had the great fortune to observe a Joanna Gleason master class, where she told us that she goes to the theatre to see real life plus one. She said she could go stand in the parking lot and watch real life. She goes to the theatre for more.

If your characters have life-altering journeys on opening night, why not let your four-minute solo show have life-altering discovery? That's a show I would to pay to see.

Vintre Scott

STEP 5: LISTEN

Now that we've come to the end of your piece, we are going to revisit a few things.

MOMENT AFTER

As you end your piece I want you to have a brief moment after. Is there more you want to say but choose not to? Is there something you wish your other would say? Did you win? Did you lose? What do you want your other to do now?

Let your piece land for a moment. So often young actors pop out of their piece so fast that it mars the moment. Stay focused on your other for a second. Silently hope for more from them. Then you can let the piece go and move on to your next thing. Just like your moment before, it should be about your other. What do you want to make your other do now? It doesn't need to be long – a second is fine, please no longer than two seconds.

RECONNECT

When you've finished your final moment after, I want you to reconnect with the person behind the table. Say thank you. You could even ask if there is more they would like to see. Do not say "scene". The word "scene" is sometimes used in monologue or scene competitions, but please do not use it in an audition. It makes you look like an amateur. Instead, look into the decision maker's eyes, connect, and read the energy of the room.

The moment right after you finish your final piece is an important moment. In this moment, you need to listen and read the energy of the room. Does the decision maker want to spend more time with you, or are you finished?

Your goal is to stay in the room as long as possible without overstaying your welcome. So often young actors finish their monologues and immediately head for the door. They obviously want out of the room. I'll be asking questions, and they just keep inching towards the door. I don't know if they think they are wasting my time or if they just want it to be over, but let me be clear: you are not wasting my time, and you want me to talk to you.

Remember, I am trying to figure out if I want to spend two years with you. Most schools are trying to figure out if they want to spend four years with you. Your audition is not all about your pieces; we are also trying to figure out who you are as a person.

If I ask you a question, don't just answer it—elaborate. For example, if I ask, "Where are you from?" you could say "Merced", or you could say, "I'm from Merced. It's not the most exciting place in the world, but it is close to a lot of cool stuff. It's only two hours to anything you'd want. Yosemite is two hours, San Francisco is two hours, the beach—two hours. It's a nice place to live, but, honestly, I'm ready for something new."

You didn't take up too much of my time, and I got to know you a bit. Remember, poised is poisonous. You are not on trial, this is your event, and you're the host. We are two equals in the room. I am not above you. You are trying to figure out if you want to spend two to four years training with me. We both have something to offer, and we both would like to get to know each other.

So, when I ask you a question, the first thing that should pop into your head is "elaborate". "What show are you working on?" You could say, "*Little Shop of Horrors*", or you could say, "I'm playing Audrey in *Little Shop of Horrors*. We're having a great time. Last fall we did *To Kill a Mockingbird*. I was in the ensemble, and the show was incredible. Let me know if you're ever in our area and would like to see one of our shows. I'd be happy to get you tickets to anything we are doing."

Let's be real, I may want to talk with you all day, but I do have to stay on schedule, so your job is to read the energy of the room. You have to be aware enough to sense the social cues. If you say "Thank you" at the end of your final piece, and I say, "Thank you. Thanks for coming in today," what does that mean? It means I've seen all I need to see, and it's time to move on. It does not mean I didn't like what you did. It just means I've seen all I need right now.

If you say "Thank you" at the end of your final piece, and I say, "Thank YOU. Yeah... huh...?" what does that mean? Hard to tell, but my energy is leading you to believe that you should stay in the room. This might be a good place to offer more. You could say, "Is there anything else I can show you?" Or you might say, "Is there anything you would like me to try differently?" The more time you spend in the room the better. Be the host. Put me at ease.

I'm sure it goes without saying, but I am going to say it anyway: if you don't have more pieces to show me, don't ask me if I would like to see anything else. I suggest you have at least one extra monologue and one extra song that you are ready to do at a moment's notice. Some colleges will tell you to have extra pieces in case they want to see more, but in most cases it is rare that you will be asked to do extra pieces at a college audition. However, if you do have extra pieces that you feel good about, you could offer more and look like a pro.

Maybe instead of saying "thank you" at the end of your final piece, you say, "Is there anything else I can do for you?" Don't wait to be asked, offer it. So often when an actor says this to me I respond with, "What else do you have?" You now have an invitation to stay in the room longer. I am going to see more of your work, and we are going to get to know each other better.

You might say, "Is there anything else I can do for you?" and I might respond with, "Yeah, let's look at your Shakespeare piece again." This is a good thing. This means I am interested, and I now want to see how well you take direction. If I ask you to do your piece again, it does not mean I did not like the way you did it the first time. It means I want to spend more time with you. I am trying to figure out if you are trainable or resistant.

When I say, "Let's do your piece again," it means I am about to give you some direction. That means you need to listen to what I am saying. Remember, you like this. You like to rehearse, you like to collaborate, so listen to what I say, and do your best to make the adjustments I am asking for right now.

For example, you may have just finished Henry V's motivational speech to his soldiers, "Once more unto the breech, dear friends, once more." I may say, "Let's do it again, but this time I want you to do it as if you are talking to a four-year-old who just woke up from a bad dream. Try to calm him and talk him back to sleep." That direction may not make a lot of sense to you. You know the givens of the play, and what I am asking you to do is ridiculous.

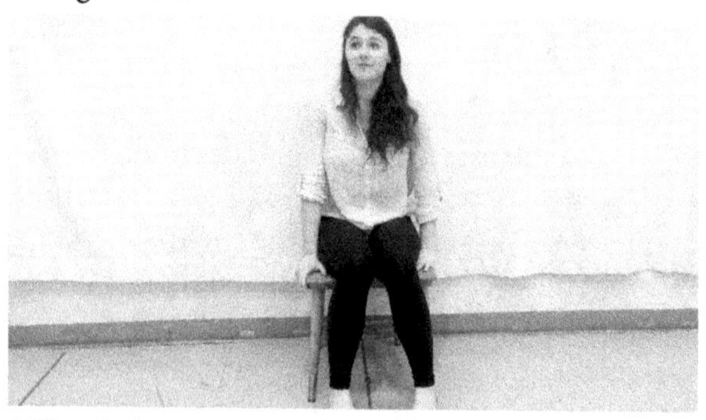

Willow Orthwein

Trust me, I am not suggesting that what you did was bad; I am not suggesting that this is how the speech should be performed in the play. What I am doing is testing you to see how well you take direction. Can you make adjustments quickly? Are you willing to try something that you don't immediately understand? Do you trust me and what my school is offering? I am trying to figure out if you are trainable.

When I ask you to do your Henry V piece again as if you are talking to a four-year-old who just woke up from a bad dream, your response needs to be, "You bet," or "Sounds great," or "Let's give it a try," or something to that effect. Then crouch down on level with a four-year-old, have a brief moment before of calmly shushing him, and then try to coax him back to sleep. "Sh, sh," (quietly and with love in your voice) "Once more unto the breech, dear friends, once more, or close the wall up with our English dead...." Have fun. Commit to it 100%. Honestly, it doesn't matter how successful the outcome is. What I need to see is your willingness to try. Your attempt is more important than the result. Make an adjustment. Show me you are willing to leap into the unknown.

If I give you direction and then you do your piece exactly as you did it before, the audition is over, and you are not getting into my school. You've just shown me that you either can't or you are not willing to take my direction. You don't trust me, and therefore I assume you are not trainable.

Please know that if I don't ask you for more, if I just say thank you and that is the end of your audition, it doesn't mean I'm not interested. It just means I've seen all I need for right now. I may have decided to call you back in the first 15 seconds of your audition. I don't need to see any more. I may be behind schedule, and I have to keep moving. You will never know what I am thinking, so don't overthink it. Just do your show, and then listen. Listen to the energy of the room. Do I want you to stay, or have I seen everything I need to see? Listen to the questions I am asking you and elaborate. Listen to the direction I am giving you and make the adjustments. Stay in the room as long as possible without overstaying your welcome.

Katie Gucik

STEP 6: MOVE ON

You've read the energy of the room, and you've sensed it is time for you to move on. I've said it before, and I will say it again: everything is better with an intention. You need to leave the room the same way you entered it - with an intention. If you have a goal, an action, an intention as you leave, then you will have something to do as you collect your music and head for the door.

I suggest you leave the room like you are going to your next audition. Your intention is to move on to the next appointment on your list. You are the host of this event. You want to avoid creating awkward situations, so leave the room with the energy of someone who has something to do. As you reach the door, maybe you turn back for one last, "Thanks again," or "Have a good day," then move on to your next appointment. The energy of someone who knows what to do is appealing. The energy of someone who knows what is next is appealing. A kind, confident person is appealing.

Sports were never really my thing. I played some soccer and

basketball; I was ok, but not great. (I know this is a tangent, but stick with me—there is a point to this story.) My dad was a very good athlete. He put himself through college on a football scholarship, and played for the army when he was stationed in Hawaii during the Korean War. Sunday and Monday nights in my house were about watching football. I found it incredibly dull and slightly annoying, because the games preempted the shows I wanted to watch, but I did like hanging out with my dad.

My favorite part of the game was when someone would score a touchdown. I grew up in the 1970's and 80's. Back then when someone scored a touchdown the team could celebrate. A player would cross the goal line, he would spike the ball, and often do a little dance. Sometimes other members of the team would run into the end zone and join the dance. Some teams would do elaborate routines when they scored a touchdown. Check out the Bear's "Superbowl Shuffle."

My dad didn't really like the touchdown celebrations. When I asked him why, his reason changed my life.

He said that when he scored touchdowns, he didn't celebrate, because he didn't want anyone to think that it was out of the ordinary for him to score touchdowns. He told me, "That's what I did. I scored touchdowns." There was no reason to make a big deal out of it, because he was going to be back in the end zone in a few minutes. When my dad scored a touchdown, he would set the ball on the ground, look at the other players, and say "I'll be back in few minutes," or "See you soon," because that's what my dad did. He scored touchdowns.

That's how I feel about auditions. There is no reason for you to make a big deal out of the audition, because this is what you do; you audition. You are prepared, you're passionate, and you have great potential. Come into my audition room, do your show, and then move on to your next audition. You love to audition. It's no big deal; this is what you do.

So often when young actors audition they feel the need to show me how they feel about how their audition went as they leave the room. Often I watch young actors sulking or reprimanding themselves as they leave the room. Apparently the audition didn't go as well as they had hoped it would. I guess they wanted me to know this, but why? Often I think the audition went well, but the person beating herself up as she leaves the room causes me to rethink what I saw. I've seen guys lose a callback because they felt the need to celebrate so loudly in the hallway that it disrupted the next audition.

Don't advertise how you feel about your audition. Just move on to the next one. This is what you do. You audition. You're a pro—move on.

Listen, you get to be happy, you get to feel bad, but wait until you are out of the building before you have a big reaction.

I'll let you in on a little secret. Your audition starts the moment you get off the freeway, and it is not over until you are back on the freeway. We are trying to figure out if we want to spend two to four years with you. People are watching you all the time.

When I am on the road auditioning, my wonderful friends and stage managers Chrissy Collins and Aleah Van Woert travel with me. They sit at a table outside my audition room and check people in. Believe me when I say they have more power than I do.

Chrissy, Aleah, and I have a code. If someone is rude, unkind, or assy in anyway, they put a particular mark on their resume. If I see that mark on someone's resume, there is nothing the person can do to get into my school. I trust Chrissy and Aleah. If they say you are not right for our school, I don't care how good your audition is, you are not getting in.

However, we also have a code for someone who is exceptionally kind, someone with a great supportive energy in the waiting room, someone who went out of their way to help a fellow auditioner. If I see the "kind code" on someone's resume, I am going to be rooting for this person. I am going to be looking for ways to accept them into my school. So be the kind person that you are. Radiate supportive energy. Help people in need.

Sierra Wells

Like I said, you get to be happy. We want you to celebrate your successes. You get to feel bad. It is ok if you think I am the biggest idiot you've ever met. Just wait until you are out of the parking lot. Get in your car, get out of the parking lot, then pull over and call someone. Scream like you just got your yellow ticket to Vegas or yell like I am the worst person you've ever met. Feel all the feels, but far away from the audition site.

I've seen too many people sabotage themselves because they made a call on their cell phone while still in the building and trashed someone they had just met.

I remember a time in Fresno. I was planning to call back a young lady who had just done what I thought was a good audition. She, apparently, was upset about it, because when she rounded the corner into the waiting room, she threw her music binder against the wall. Chrissy saw her do this, and reported it to me. I later found out that she was upset because her friend got called back on the spot, but she didn't.

What she didn't know was that I see five women for every one guy. Sometimes I can call back a guy right after his audition while he is still in the room, because I don't have as many guys to choose from. It is more challenging when auditioning ladies. I have so many young women who audition for the Conservatory. I have to wait until all the auditions are finished before I can decide which ladies I can invite to callbacks. It is not fair, but if you are looking for fair, I suggest you pursue a different career. The young lady's friend was a guy. I called him back on the spot. I thought the young lady was quite good; I was planning to call her back, but then she acted like a tool, and I changed my mind.

A few years ago I was holding auditions in LA. I was setting up tables in the waiting room, and I still had my jacket on. A guy walked into the waiting room and rudely demanded to know if this was where the auditions were. I said yes, and he said with disdain in his voice, "Well, you should put up some signs or something. This is really hard to find." He thought he was talking to someone who worked for the building, and he apparently thought it was okay to be rude to the building staff. I said to the man that I would be sure to get some signs up and make it easier for people to find. He rolled his eyes, and then I took off my jacket revealing a name badge that said "Casting Director". His eyes got huge. He realized he had just yelled at the decision maker. I then walked into the audition room and said, "Next." He walked in sheepishly, knowing he had just been an ass. He might as well have just turned around and left, because he showed me who he really was when he was rude to what he thought was the "help." And as Dr. Maya Angelou says, "When someone shows you who they are, believe them."

Everyone is on their best behavior around the recruiter or the casting director. I want to know what you are like when I am not around, so I have spies everywhere. Your audition begins the moment you get off the freeway, and it doesn't end until you are back on the freeway.

The vast majority of those who audition for me are kind, wonderful people. Sometimes someone can show their insecure side when they are uncomfortable or they don't know what to do. Well, there is no reason for you to be insecure or uncomfortable. You are prepared, and you are passionate. You are the host of this event. Be your wonderfully kind, authentic self throughout the whole process. Connect with people, share your light, support your fellow artists, be focused, and be a pro. This is what you do; you audition.

YOUR FIRST ENTRANCE

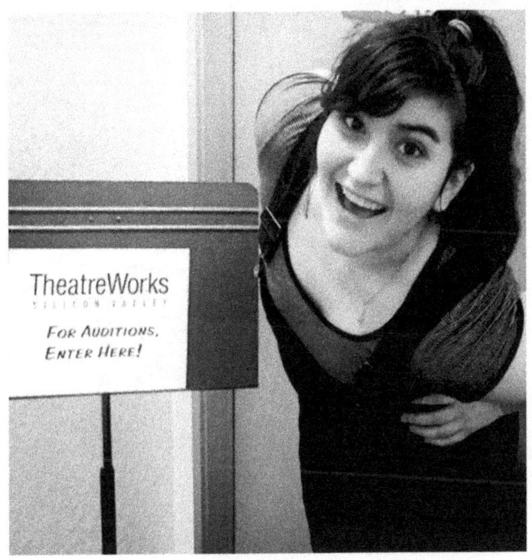

Maya Sherer

TO YOUR FINAL EXIT

YOUR FIRST ENTRANCE TO YOUR FINAL EXIT

Now you know the steps necessary to create a four minute solo show that I should pay to see. Let's talk through the whole thing from your first entrance to your final exit.

You are in the hallway (the wings) waiting to walk through the door into the audition room (the stage). Think through the steps. This is your event, and you are the host. You want to put the decision maker (me) at ease. You enter the room with the intention to connect with me.

As you walk in the room you smile and say, "Hello" or "Hi" or "Good morning" or "Thanks for seeing me." You try to look into my eyes. You want your eyes to look into my eyes.

You cross to the piano and try to connect with the accompanist. You smile and say "Hello" or "Hi" or "Thanks for playing for me." Place your music on the piano open to the first page of your song. Let the accompanist know where you plan to start and where you plan stop. Give them your tempo by singing a few bars of your song, and point out any surprises in your song.

Say "Thank you" to the accompanist and cross to the center of the room while trying to connect with me. Smile, look into my eyes, and introduce yourself. Say your name clearly, let me know the first piece you plan to do, your second piece, and your song. Continue to try to connect.

> **Note:** I like it when actors introduce all of their pieces at the beginning of the audition. This allows me to write everything down and then sit back and enjoy your show. However, it is also acceptable to introduce as you go. You could introduce your first piece then do it, introduce your second piece then do it, and so on. It's your show. Create what you would want to see and then do it.

After you finish your introduction, find your target and be very clear who your other is. Let your other affect you and have a brief yet obvious moment before. Fight to change your other, make a discovery and deal with the unexpected by changing your tactics. The piece ends with a brief moment after. What more do you want from your other?

Now let the first piece go, find a new target and repeat: Clear other, obvious moment before, discovery, new tactic, brief moment after.

Let go of your second piece. Look to the accompanist to let them know you are ready to sing. As they start to play, make sure you have a clear target for your other. Inhale your obvious moment before, and sing to change your other. Make a discovery, change your tactics, and have a brief moment after.

> **Note:** I suggest you target your other to one side of the decision maker or the other. Don't go too far to the side. I want to see your face for the majority of the piece not your profile. If there is more than one decision maker behind the table, you can target your other between the decision makers. I suggest that your first piece is to one side, your second piece is to the other side, and your third piece is your choice.

Transitioning from piece to piece is part of your show. Rehearse these transitions, so that they can be clear and efficient. We need to know that one piece has ended and the next one is about to begin. We don't need the word "scene"; we don't need you to drop your head.

We just need you to let go of your moment after and then find a new target. No need to rush; just be efficient.

After you finish your final piece, reconnect with me behind the table. Try to look into my eyes, smile, and say "Thank you" or "Is there anything else I can do for you?" Read the energy of the room. Do I want more or is it time for you to move on to your next audition? If I ask you questions, listen, then elaborate. If I ask you to do your piece again, listen to my direction and then commit to making the adjustment.

Stay in the room as long as possible without overstaying your welcome.

Once it is clear that I have seen everything I need from you, smile and say "Thank you" or "It was great to meet you." Cross to the piano and get your music. Thank the accompanist. Cross to the door with the intention of moving on to your next audition, and, as you exit the room, turn back for one last "Thanks again."

Madison Davis

There is no reason auditioning should be scary. You like to do this. You like to get up in front of people and perform. You have the tools, and you have the talent. Now all you have to do is prepare. Follow the steps and rehearse, so you have the confidence to let me see your authentic passion. Create the solo show you would want to see if you were the decision maker sitting behind the table. Make me want to pay you. This is your opening night, and the unknown is thrilling. No Caution!

PART 3:
THINGS TO CONSIDER

ba da bum bum bum bum bum
doo doo
doo doo doo
bum bum
bum bum
concert
please
the rest
Kurete

PART 3: THINGS TO CONSIDER

The following section touches on a few things I suggest you consider when putting together your solo show. These suggestions are meant to give you the advantage of looking like a pro when auditioning for universities, colleges, conservatories, and beyond.

MATERIAL

Choosing audition material that shows you off will be a career-long challenge. Actors are always looking for the perfect monologues and the perfect songs. It can be frustrating. You need to find something that showcases your essence as an actor – something that shows your marketability (where you are most castable) and also shows your skill set and your potential. It is also in your best interest to find material that is not overdone.

Be on the constant lookout for good, sophisticated material. Go see everything. Read plays whenever possible. During your summer break, challenge yourself to read a play a week. If it was nominated for something, read it. Go see plays at all of the schools in your area. Sign up to usher at your local community theatre and/or professional theatre. It does not matter if the play is well produced. You can find good material even if it is not well performed.

> **Note:** It is very important to go see theatre. How can we expect people to come see our shows if we don't go? You can learn so much by watching others perform. Most of what I know I learned from watching people better than me. However, I have also learned a lot by watching performances that did not meet my expectations. You will be better when you can articulate why you liked something and when you can identify why you did not. I love being in the theater—just being in the building. I want to be around it all the time. If you don't enjoy going to see shows, then I don't see how you can have a life in this industry. Go see everything!

Many schools will require that you choose material from a published play or musical. This frustrates me, however, these are the rules, and I strongly suggest you follow them. If they do not specify that your monologue must be from a published play, then look for sophisticated material everywhere.

> **Rant:** I believe good writing is good writing. I don't care where you find your monologue if it is well written. I don't understand why it is okay to do a monologue from the play *Other Dessert Cities* by John Robin Baitz, but it is not okay to do a monologue from the TV show *Brothers and Sisters* by John Robin Baitz. Aaron Sorkin is one of the best writers we have in America. His plays are good, but his TV and film writing is better. Why is it more acceptable to choose a monologue from his play *The Farnsworth Invention* than from his brilliant HBO series *The Newsroom*? I believe the rules that material must come from a published play are outdated. They are relics from a time when many looked down on TV. I love the theatre, I've made my life in the theatre, and we live in a time when some of the best writing is on TV and

> in films. Many of our best playwrights now write for TV and films. The idea that monologues must come from a published play is archaic, and I think this rule will change soon. However, until it does change, be sure to be very aware of the requirements and the instructions listed by each school that interests you.

If the school does not specify that your monologue must come from a published play, and you decide to do a piece from TV or film, you have to be smart about your selection. I suggest you avoid extremely popular TV shows and movies. You do not want the decision maker immediately associating your monologue with a famous person. If you do Samuel L. Jackson's opening monologue from *Pulp Fiction*, most decision makers will recognize it immediately and think about Samuel L. Jackson instead of you. (The same way people think about Judy Garland whenever they hear *Somewhere Over the Rainbow*.) Sometimes just saying the title of the film or TV show can cause the decision maker to form an opinion before you do your show. For example, if you say you are doing a piece from the TV show *Friends*, I immediately start thinking about Lisa Kudrow, Matt LeBlanc, and the rest of the gang. Maybe you don't introduce your monologue with the title of the TV show. You could introduce it with the title of the episode. I loved the TV show *Scrubs*, but I don't know it well enough to immediately recognize a monologue from it. Instead of introducing the monologue as a piece from *Scrubs*, look up the title of the episode. (The title of the first episode of *Scrubs* is *My First Day*.) You could introduce a movie by saying you will be doing a "piece by (insert author's name)" instead of saying the title of the movie. I also suggest you find the transcript for the show or movie online instead of writing it down by listening to it over and over. I want to see your interpretation of this character; I don't want to watch you imitate someone else's performance.

Don't just look at what is popular now; look at films and TV shows from ten, twenty... fifty years ago. I've had great success with a monologue I got from the 90's TV show *Mad About You*. My wife has a wonderful piece from the 80's movie *Soap Dish*. Think strategically. Find the writing that showcases your potential without undermining you with its title or popularity.

No matter where you are looking, challenge yourself to find sophisticated material. Look at material that is or was nominated for awards—Tony awards, Obie awards, Outer Critics awards, Academy awards, SAG awards, Writers Guild awards, Emmy awards, Peabody awards, Pulitzer Prize Awards....

I also suggest you work on characters who are close to your age. Show me something that you could play now or in the next five to ten years.

I recommend you avoid finding your monologue on the internet. Every year I can guess which monologues come up first in a google search. It becomes very apparent quickly which are the top three female monologues on the internet. I promise you, if you found your monologue on the internet, so did thousands of other young actors.

I think it is important to be aware of what material is overdone, but don't obsess about it. Yes, *Dog Sees God* is overdone. I'm personally not a fan, and I would rather not see pieces from it. But, it is your show. You need to show me what you want to show me. Don't get caught up in trying to guess what I like and what I don't. "Pulled" from *The Addams Family* is also overdone, yet I never seem to tire of it. Figure out what you like, examine the givens of the piece, let those givens inform your own personal take on the piece, rehearse, and then show me your opening night. No caution!

Narrative monologues can be a challenge. A narrative monologue is a monologue that talks about something that already happened. We touched on this earlier. I want to see you do more than report information. I want you to make life-altering discovery during your solo show. I want to watch you put a puzzle together. That is hard to do if you are telling me about something that already happened. I suggest you avoid monologues that are mostly talking about things that already happened. For example, a narrative monologue might sound something like this:

> *When I was a kid, I had a dog. He was a great dog. He was yellow, some sort of Lab mix, he was basically perfect, and we used to love to go on long walks in the woods behind my house. One day we were out walking, and he just stopped. He wouldn't budge, and then suddenly he started digging. He was digging and*

digging—he was obviously very excited. I'd never seen him act like this before....

This might be an interesting story, but it would be hard to do more than just report information. You might be able to report it in an interesting way, but it would be very difficult to find discovery. Where does the pebble drop? I am not saying it's impossible, there are exceptions to most every rule. However, if you want to have a moment before, if you want to fight to make your other do something right now, if you want to have discovery and deal with something unexpected... that is a lot harder to do with a narrative monologue.

Note: Some monologues start narrative and then switch to the present tense. These can be effective, but remember, we form an opinion quickly when watching your solo show. I want to see you fighting to change your other—fighting to win. Don't live in narrative too long.

I think young actors often choose to show me narrative monologues because those tend to be the longer or chunkier speeches when looking at a script. Some young actors look for monologues by getting scripts and flipping through them looking for longer speeches. When they come to a chunk of text, they stop and read it and decide if they like it. That's what unsophisticated actors do. If you want to stand out, if you want to be perceived as a pro, you need to read plays and think outside the box.

I think the best way to find monologues is to read plays and gravitate towards two person scenes where one person is dominating most of the scene. So many plays have scenes where one person is doing most of the talking and the other person is occasionally interrupting with one or two words. If you were just flipping through the script, it wouldn't look like a monologue, but if you took out the lines where the other person is interrupting, it would become a monologue. For example:

A scene between Teresa and Joel from my play *Silent Night Holy $#*+*:

TERESA

Am I late? Oh, God, I'm late. Have you guys started yet? I can't believe this! My first day, and I'm late! I'm so sorry. It won't happen again.

KEN

It's ten 'till. You've got ten minutes.

TERESA

Sue said being on time meant being here fifteen minutes early. A professional actor always arrives early so that he or she is warmed up and ready.

KEN

Yeah, well, Sue's not here yet, so I think you're going to be fine.

TERESA

It's just that when I was a Beefy Buddy we arrived at our scheduled time. We didn't need to warm up. We just needed to set up. But as Sue says, I am no longer a Beefy Buddy, and I need to remember that. I'm going to do a quick warm up, but I'm ready any time. You guys just let me know. Ok, because I'm right here.

KEN

Ok, well, we just thought we would wait for the rest of the cast and the director.

TERESA

That's fine, that's fine. (*Runs into Joel*) Hi. I'm Teresa.

JOEL

I'm Joel, Joel Kneedler.

TERESA

Merry Christmas.

JOEL

Merry....

TERESA

I mean Happy Holidays.

JOEL

Oh...ah... Happy....

TERESA

I didn't mean to say Merry Christmas.

JOEL

It's fine.

TERESA

You might be Jewish.

JOEL

I'm not....

TERESA

Or maybe you're nothing.

JOEL

Merry Christmas is fine. I like Christmas. I'm actually looking forward to doing a Christmas show.

TERESA

Me too. I guess we're the virgins.

JOEL

In the show?! Is that in the script?

TERESA

We're the new cast members.

JOEL

Oh, right.

TERESA

I didn't mean we were virgins.

JOEL

Of course not.
(*Beat*)

TERESA

You might be a virgin.

JOEL

No!

TERESA

That'd be fine.

JOEL

Of course.

TERESA

But I wouldn't know.

JOEL

Right.
(*Beat*)

TERESA

I'm not a virgin.

JOEL

Ok.

TERESA

(*Quickly*) I mean, I haven't slept with that many people.

JOEL

I'm sure....

But I have had sex.

JOEL

Fine. That's fine.
(*Beat*)

TERESA

Three times. I've had sex three times, but I don't think that that's too many.

JOEL

Me neither.

TERESA

I just meant it was our first time at The Prime Rib Playhouse.

JOEL

So this is your first time working here.

TERESA

No

JOEL

But you just said....

TERESA

I used to be a Beefy Buddy.

Now let's turn it into a monologue:

TERESA

Am I late? Oh, God, I'm late. Have you guys started yet? I can't believe this! My first day, and I'm late! I'm so sorry. It won't happen again. Sue said being on time meant being here fifteen minutes early. A professional actor always arrives early so that he or she is warmed up and ready. It's just that when I was a Beefy Buddy we arrived at our scheduled time. We didn't need to warm up. We just needed to set up. But as Sue says, I am no longer a Beefy Buddy, and I need to remember that. I'm going to do a quick warm up, but I'm ready any time. You just let me know. Ok, because I'm right here. I'm Teresa. Merry Christmas. (*Realizing her mistake*) I mean Happy Holidays. I didn't mean to say Merry Christmas. You might be Jewish. Or maybe you're nothing. (*Pause*) I like Christmas. I'm actually looking forward to doing the Christmas show. I guess we're the virgins. (*Clarifying*) We're the new cast members. I didn't mean we were virgins. (*Beat*) You might be a virgin. That'd be fine. But I wouldn't know. (*Beat*) I'm not a virgin. (*Urgently clarifying*) I mean, I haven't slept with that many people. But I have had sex. (*Beat*) Three times. I've had sex three times, but I don't think that that's too many. (*Pause*) I just meant it was our first time at The Prime Rib Playhouse. (*Beat*) I used to be a Beefy Buddy.

I took a scene and turned it into a monologue. I just took out the other character's lines. I even took one of Joel's lines and made it Teresa's. You can do whatever you want. It is your show. You can change a line or word. You can take another character's line and make it yours. You could cut several lines. You could move lines and put them where you need them. It is your show.

> **Note:** I highly recommend you do not change or alter well-known, famous, iconic plays. For example, I would not alter Stanley from *A Street Car Named Desire* or a scene from *All My Sons*. These plays are

so well known, the viewer might stop watching you and start wondering what you have done to this very famous piece of literature.

Here is another example:

FIRST MURDERER
Make peace with God, for you must die, my lord.

CLARENCE
Hast thou that holy feeling in thy soul,
To counsel me to make my peace with God,
And art thou yet to thy own soul so blind,
That thou wilt war with God by murdering me?
Ah, sirs, consider, he that set you on
To do this deed will hate you for the deed.

SECOND MURDERER
What shall we do?

CLARENCE
Relent, and save your souls.

FIRST MURDERER
Relent! 'tis cowardly and womanish.

CLARENCE
Not to relent is beastly, savage, devilish.
Which of you, if you were a prince's son,
Being pent from liberty, as I am now,
If two such murderers as yourselves came to you,
Would not entreat for life?
My friend, I spy some pity in thy looks:
O, if thine eye be not a flatterer,
Come thou on my side, and entreat for me,
As you would beg, were you in my distress
A begging prince what beggar pities not?

Now let's turn it into a monologue:

CLARENCE
Hast thou that holy feeling in thy soul,
To counsel me to make my peace with God,
And art thou yet to thy own soul so blind,
That thou wilt war with God by murdering me?
Ah, sirs, consider, he that set you on
To do this deed will hate you for the deed.
Relent, and save your souls.
Not to relent is beastly, savage, devilish.
Which of you, if you were a prince's son,
Being pent from liberty, as I am now,
If two such murderers as yourselves came to you,
Would not entreat for life?
My friend, I spy some pity in thy looks:
O, if thine eye be not a flatterer,
Come thou on my side, and entreat for me,
As you would beg, were you in my distress
A begging prince what beggar pities not?

This is from Shakespeare's *Richard III.* It is pretty famous, but we didn't really alter anything. We just took out the other characters' lines and made two short pieces and one line into one longer piece. We were even able to stay true to the verse and honor the rhythm of the poetry.

I highly recommend that once you turn a scene into a monologue you do not pretend to hear your scene partner's lines. It can be confusing for the viewer if you are pretending that the other person is speaking. I don't want to watch one half of a dialogue. If you pause for and then react to a line from your other, we then have to figure out what the line was that we didn't hear. We stop listening to you and start trying to fill in the blanks.

Instead, play the monologue as if your other is not speaking, or play it as if you are not letting your other speak. You could even have a moment where you play that you already know what your other is going to say and you are not going to let them say it. If you need their line to make the next moment make sense, you could say something like, "I know, I know you want me to shut up, but I refuse." Or, "Yeah, yeah, everyone thinks my life is easy, but it's not." If you can make it work without adding a line, I suggest you do, but if you need it, do it. It's your show.

Think outside the box. Craft the piece you find to fit what you need. If you find the perfect piece that works without any alterations, that is great. But if you find a scene that could be a great monologue if you just alter it, do it. No caution!!

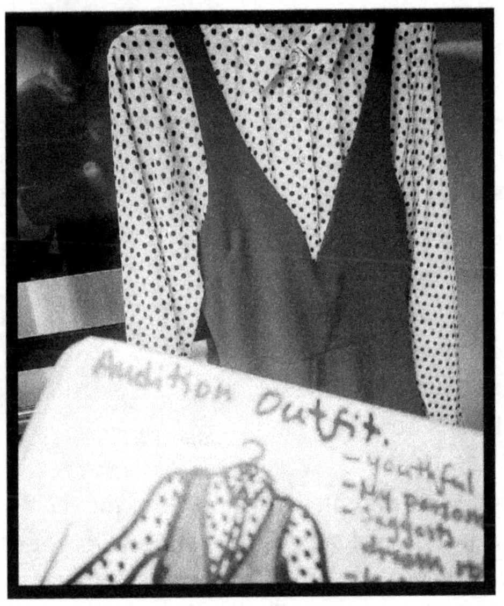

WHAT TO WEAR?

Sometimes someone will audition for me, and I get sad, because I can only assume by what they are wearing that they have no friends. No true friend would ever have let that person show up looking like that. Some people do not look good in an empire waist dress, and they need a real friend to tell them the truth. We all need to have that group of friends who will be honest with us. Rock stars have their squad. You should too.

Meami Maszewski, Natalia Womack, Bianca Norwood, Cheyenne Omani

You need to have that friend who you can try on outfits with, or skype with, or text pictures to. And you need to make sure they will tell you the truth. Don't ask your boyfriend if these pants make your butt look big. If he has any brains at all, he will respond without hesitation that you look amazing in everything.

I'm not sure your mom or dad are the best people to help you pick out your outfit. Your parents have a particular vision of you that may be what you were instead of what you are. I'm 48 years old and my mom still doesn't like the resume pictures my agent picked. She says that I am sweeter than what my pictures show. Well, yes, I am sweet, but that is not what I am marketing.

Bianca Norwood and Ella Ruth Francis

I understand your parents may be paying for the outfit, so they may get to have some say. I suggest you shop with your friends first, and then show your parents only the options you want them to see: the options you picked out with feedback from your squad.

I am no fashion guru, but I do have some insight into picking out the right audition outfit.

Some say that your audition is a job interview, and you should dress with that in mind. I don't disagree, but I would go further.

First of all, this is your show, and you need to think about how your clothes can help your opening night. Remember, poised is poisonous. If you dress like you work at Office Max, how am I going to get any sense of who you are?

I am not suggesting you dress in an outrageous manner. You want the decision makers sitting behind the desk to watch your work. You do not want them to be distracted by your clothing. Yet, dressing in a way that highlights the best of who you are can make a wonderful impression as you walk through the door.

I suggest you ask yourself a couple of questions when picking out your outfit:

> What would you wear if you were meeting your boyfriend's or girlfriend's parents for the first time?

I imagine you would want to look nice. You may not want to overdo it, but you don't want to undersell yourself either. You don't want to show too much skin, but you also want to be comfortable. You don't want to make such a huge statement with your clothes that that's all they remember, yet you do want them to get to know the real you. I imagine you would like your outfit to add to the experience, yet not dominate the experience.

> What would you wear to a first date? However, it is a lunch date. You are not looking for action; you are just hoping for a second date.

An audition has some similarities to a first date. We don't know each other. We are putting our best foot forward, so we can get to know each other. We are trying to figure out if we would like to meet again and get to know each other better.

I imagine you'd put some thought into what you might wear on a first date. You want to look nice. You want to show a bit of who you are, a bit of your personality. You would like to be appealing, yet you don't want to look too eager or scandalous.

Those of us behind the desk have a bit of an ego. We like to think you put some effort into preparing for this event. I want to feel worth your time. I'd like to feel like you picked out these pieces just for me, and you chose this outfit specifically for this show. I know it's not true. I know you are auditioning for a lot of decision makers, but it is nice when I feel like you created your show just for me.

It is not uncommon for me to wonder if the actor slept in the clothes they decided to wear to the audition. They show up in what appears to be dirty jeans and a wrinkly T-shirt. They might even say something like, "My friend told me about this audition. I don't really know what it's for." Even if that is true, why would you tell me? I don't want to feel like an afterthought. I want to feel worth your time.

So, yes, this is a job interview. Be a pro. This is also your event, and you are the host. Let me see a bit of you in what you decide to wear.

Guys, you kind of have it easy. You just need to look like you made an effort. If you iron what you wear, you are going to be in the top twenty percent. The bar for guys is not high. You could wear nice pants or a good pair of jeans. You could wear a button up dress shirt, a polo shirt, or a well-fitted clean T shirt. You could wear a tie, you could loosen it, or not wear it at all. You could wear dress shoes or clean sneakers. You just have to decide what suits your show the best. Personally, I think solid colors work best. Maybe you wear nice jeans, a black t-shirt, and a dress shirt with the top two or three buttons undone. Comb your hair, wear clean shoes, and you are good to go.

A lot of young women ask me if they should wear pants, a skirt, or a dress. All I can tell you is that all of these options can work. Many young women wear pants or leggings with a long shirt or tunic. Maybe they wear a belt. Many wear a nice summer dress. Some wear a skirt, blouse, and a cardigan sweater. Some wear a dress and leggings.... There are so many options. It is your show, so you should costume it the way you think is best. It might be fun to imagine someone else is playing you in your life story. How would you costume that actor to play you on a first date? Remember, it is a lunch date.

I strongly recommend you don't show too much skin or wear a low cut top. You want us to watch you and your work. You do not want us to be distracted by what you wear, and you do not want us to worry that we are going to see something we shouldn't.

If you decide to wear a dress or a skirt, I strongly recommend you wear bike shorts or leggings under your dress. We might ask you to do your piece crouched down or sitting on the floor. We might ask you to physicalize your piece, and you do not want to feel limited.

Think about your foundation garments. Can we see them through what you are wearing? Are there lines or seams that distract? Are the straps too thin? Would a sports bra be better? Are spanx a good idea? These types of questions would be great questions to ask your squad.

What shoes are you going to wear? Make sure they are part of the story you want to tell, and wear them while you rehearse. You need to be very comfortable in these shoes.

Sometimes people alter their look during their solo show. I think this can work well as long as it is efficient and simple. For example, maybe you wear a tie for your first piece, loosen it for your second piece, and take it off during your third piece. You could wear a nice cardigan for your first piece, and tie it around your waist for your second piece, and around your shoulders for your third piece. You could wear your heels for your first two pieces, but kick them off and be barefoot for your song.

I suggest you take things off as you go instead of entering carrying something you are going to put on later. For example, if you want to do one of your pieces barefoot, then do it last. It is much easier to kick off your shoes than it is to put them on. You can always exit carrying your shoes and put them back on in the hall.

I once saw a wonderful actor who came in wearing a lovely shawl over her shoulders. She did her first piece, then she put the shawl up on her head and did another piece, then she tied it around her waist for her song. This makes me feel like I am watching a show. It was simple and efficient. It added to the transition from piece to piece, but the pieces didn't become all about the shawl.

Maria Centrella, Joshua Ponce, Sophia Caressa, Tiago Santos, Bailey Leyvas, Daniel Geiger, Parker Harris

What it really comes down to is that we want your outfit to enhance your show, not dominate your show. Be a pro, be you, look good, yet avoid things that distract. I suggest you avoid dangling earrings and necklaces that make too big of a statement. I love polka dots, yet I would be carful of prints that get too busy. You might want to avoid clothes with writing or someone else's face. You don't want me reading your shirt while you are auditioning.

There is a wonderful movie from the 90's called *Clueless*. In *Clue-*

less, the main character, Cher, is truly a fashion guru. She selects her outfits with great care, and then, just as she is about to leave for her event, she turns back for one quick glance in the mirror. Whatever accessory catches her eye first, she takes off. She wants people to see her, not her baubles. Her clothes are meant to enhance not distract.

Brittany Law

THE SHOW MUST GO ON

It's rare that things go wrong on the audition day, but we should talk about it just in case. I think it is always good to have a plan, and then let it go when you don't need it.

What happens if on the day of your audition you wake up super sick and you have no voice? I think the best way to approach this is to ask yourself, "What would you do if this was opening night?" Would you cancel the show?

If you are so sick that you would have to cancel the show, then you need to contact the decision makers that are planning to see you that day, and let them know that you have to cancel. Tell them that you are so sorry for the inconvenience, but you are very sick, and ask them if there is any way you can reschedule or send a video audition. It is very important that you call and/or email the decision makers. I recommend you do both. I can be very understanding if you communicate with me, but if you just don't show up, if you don't call or email, I am finished with you.

Rant: When you don't show up, it's a big deal. When I am on the road holding auditions for PCPA, about 25% of the actors who make an appointment don't show up. They don't call, they don't email; they just don't show up. I have limited spots available for actors who want to audition. A lot of people who want to audition for me can't because all of the audition slots are full.

When you don't show up, that is a wasted opportunity not just for you, but for the actor who wanted that slot and couldn't get it. When you don't show up, it really pisses me off.

Having integrity means you are going to do what you say you're going to do when you say you're going to do it. You need to decide what type of person you want to be. Are you a person who lives in the center of their integrity or are you a flake? Professionals show up when they say they are going to show up, and they are ready to do what they say they are going to do. I want to work with a pro, not someone who is flakey.

On the Bright Side: If you can't get an appointment, because all of the time slots are full, I strongly recommend you still show up. Chances are some people who had appointments will not show up, and the decision makers will be able to squeeze you in. Show up early, let them know you were not able to get an appointment, and you would like to get on the waiting list. If you get there a half hour early, if you are ready to go at a moment's notice, and you can wait for a few hours, most decision makers will find a way to see you.

Bianca Norwood

Most actors I know will do everything in their power to make sure the show can go on, and I know you are the same. So what do you do if you wake up on the morning of your audition, and you don't feel well?

Chances are if you can stand, you can do your monologues.

What if you view your symptoms as a gift? What if the aches and pains of the flu are just another obstacle your character has to overcome as they fight to win. What if that chest congestion is just another obstacle as you deal with the unexpected? Use yourself in your work.

I recently worked with a truly gifted young actor who had some challenges at home. Her mother struggled with alcohol. Often when this young actor came home at night, her mother would be passed out on the floor. When she finally confronted her mother about it, her mother changed the locks on the house without telling her. She came home from the State Thespian Festival to find her key no longer worked.

She decided that she was going to go live with her father in a different town. This was a really hard decision; she didn't want to leave her mother. She had been taking care of her for years. She had basically been the mom in the household, however, the time had come for her to take care of herself.

I had been coaching her on Louise's monologue from *Gypsy*—the one near the end where she finally stands up to Mama Rose. She had always done a good job with the monologue; she had been able to use herself—her life in the piece. However, the day we worked on it when she was sick was magical. She was exhausted and in pain, and she used it.

I had been trying to break through the armor she had up. I was trying to help her find how vulnerable Louise is as she finally stands up to her mother. It is scary to finally admit that you love yourself—that you love yourself enough to remove someone from your life who you love but is toxic. It wasn't until she was sick that the armor came down. She just didn't have the energy to hide. She was so exhausted, and through that exhaustion she experienced vulnerability for the first time.

From that moment on, whenever she did the monologue, she could pull from that experience of being sick. She could fight through the exhaustion of a life lived with her mother, open her heart, discover that she loved herself, and plead with her mother to let her go. She used herself (her life experiences and the reality of how she was feeling that day) and her piece became more layered, more sophisticated, more vulnerable, more real. I might also add that she got twenty callbacks at the National Thespian Festival.

Does this mean you should try to get sick while you are working on your solo show? Of course not. What it does mean is that you should bring yourself to your pieces. If you are sick on the day of your audition, use it. It may shine a light on something you've never considered before.

However...

Singing while you are sick can be a challenge. It's easy for me to say the show must go on, but if you wake up and you are so sick you can't hit the notes, what do you do?

Recruitment season happens during flu season, so having a plan is a good idea. I recommend you talk to your coach about a second song or a backup song that you can sing no matter what.

For example, what do you do if you are planning to sing "If I Can't Love Her" from *Beauty and the Beast*, but when you wake up on the day of the audition you just can't manage the F at the end of the song? Well, if you're a pro, you've got a backup song—a safety song—a song like "Tonight at Eight" from *She Loves Me*—a simple song, with a small range, and no sustained notes, but a great acting song. Show me what a great singing actor you are. I would much rather hear you sing and act an easy song well than attempt a challenging song when you can't hit the notes.

I don't care how much you love it when Billy Joel sings "Piano Man." If he's sick, and he can't hit the notes, you don't want to hear him sing it.

Your solo show is the time to show me what you do well. If you wake up and can't sing the song you planned, change your show and show me something you can sing well.

> **Note:** Do not tell me you're sick, and don't try to show me by coughing or amplifying other symptoms. This is the opening night of your solo show, and I am your audience. Would you tell the audience on opening night of *She Kills Monsters* that you're sick? Would you walk out on stage before the performance and make an announcement? Would you cough through the show, so the audience knows you're sick? Of course not. Be a pro. Don't spin in the obstacle of being sick. Instead, fight to overcome your illness. Fight to win.

If you are feeling ill during audition season, or you are afraid you might get sick, here are a few things that help me stay healthy. These are things that work for me. I don't know if they are necessarily right for you. I strongly recommend you consult a physician before you try anything new.

- I get a flu shot every year in October. The flu shot works for me. If you decide it is right for you, please remember that it takes a few weeks to start working. If you plan to get one, get it early, so it is in full effect by recruitment season.

- I make sure I am getting enough sleep. I prioritize getting 8 hours of sleep every night before and during recruitment season.

- I drink a lot of water. I make sure to drink at least 64 ounces (approximately 8 glasses) every day. Water not only helps me stay healthy, it is very good for my voice. I stay hydrated!

- I always boost my vitamin C before, during, and after my

audition trips—especially if I am flying anywhere. People often get sick after they fly because of the recycled air on airplanes.

- Ginger, Garlic, and Apple Cider Vinegar are good for my voice. When my voice is tired, I drink very strong ginger tea, I chew a raw clove of garlic, and I drink a glass of water with a tablespoon of apple cider vinegar in it. (Not all at once.)

- Ricola cough drops help my tired voice, but I think Vocal Zone cough drops are the best. I avoid any cough drops that have menthol in them. They dry out my voice.

- Glycerin is good for my voice. When I am singing a lot in a show, I add some glycerin to my backstage water bottle. I also keep Gummy Bears with me. Seriously, I find them to be very soothing for my voice, and they make me happy.

- I am very careful about which allergy and cold medicine I take. Claritin and allergy meds like Claritin dry me out and affect my voice. I find medicines that contain Guaifenesin do not dry me out.

- Don't smoke and do not vape.

TRAFFIC OR YOU'RE LOST

On opening night, if there is a chance you might get lost on your way to the theater, or you might encounter traffic, you leave early. Treat your audition the same way. Check traffic trends, know the route you plan to take to the audition venue, and leave early. Plan to get to the audition site 40 minutes early. This gives you a cushion in case you get lost or encounter unexpected traffic. If everything goes smoothly and you arrive 40 minutes early, then you can think through your show one last time. You can find the restroom and make sure your outfit, hair, and make-up look good. You can sit and breathe for a moment.

Hint: Don't let the person checking in people outside the room know you are there until you are truly ready to go. Sometimes decision makers get ahead of schedule. If you let them know you are there, they may ask you to go early. If they ask you to go early, you want to say yes, but you also want to be ready. So if you want to think through your show, and/or use the restroom, do it before you let them know you've arrived. Once you are ready, check in with the person outside the room. Then if they ask you if you would like to go early, you can say, "Sure" with ease and confidence, because this is what you do. You audition.

Make sure you have contact information for the decision makers and/or the audition venue with you - even if it is just the contact information for the person you've been emailing to set up your appointment. If you do get lost or hit traffic, and it looks like you might be late, call and/or email the decision makers. I am very grateful when people let me know they are running late. I will go out of my way to help someone who takes the time to communicate with me.

WHAT DO YOU DO IF YOU MESS UP?

This is a hard question. The easy answer is that this is the opening night of your solo show. You don't stop on opening night if things aren't going well and ask to start over.

My recommendation is if you can keep going do so. If you skip a section in your monologue or you sing the wrong verse of your song, just keep going. That's what you would do on opening night.

But... if you start singing, and you and the accompanist are in different keys, or the tempo is so off you won't be able to get through the song, or you skipped so much of your Shakespeare monologue that it is now only four lines long, then it might be best to start over.

No need to apologize—this is your show. Just stop and say, "I'm going to start again." If there is trouble at the piano, DO NOT BLAME THE ACCOMPANIST—even if it is obviously the accompanist's fault. You take the blame and say, "I wasn't clear with the accompanist. Let me check in with them, and then we will start again."

Let me repeat, do not ***ever*** blame the accompanist. And do not look at or glare at the accompanist while you're singing. Do not try to indicate that the accompanist is doing something wrong. You wouldn't do that on opening night, don't do it in your audition. Just stay focused on trying to change your other, make discoveries, and let me watch your character deal with the unexpected.

Years ago, I was recruiting and casting at a combined audition. (A combined audition is where a group of theatres or schools come together in one location and actors audition for all of the schools or theatres at one time. For example, you stand on stage and do your solo show while fifty schools or theatres sit in the audience and watch. The "Unifieds" are the most well known college combined audition.)

A young man entered this combined audition with confidence, his monologue was great, and I thought his song went well. He was probably the best person I had seen all day. It looked like just about every recruiter and casting director was going to call him back. The accompanist started to stand up as the young man was exiting, and the young man whispered something to him as he walked by. The accompanist announced to all in the room that he had been going to tell us that he had not played the young man's song well and to please consider that when evaluating his performance, but instead he thought he should tell us that the young man had just whispered to him, "Thanks for #$@%ing up my audition." The accompanist then sat back down, and the young man got zero callbacks.

The accompanist is your advocate. They can be your best friend in your audition. Treat them well—treat them as you would want to be treated.

Do the work you need to do to make sure your show can go on no matter what you encounter on the day of the audition. If unexpected obstacles arise that may cause you to be late or miss your audition, communicate. The decision makers are rooting for you. We are on your side, and we want you to be exactly what we are looking for. We will do what we can to help as long as you are prepared and you communicate.

I WILL LIKE YOU EVEN MORE IF YOU...

WRITE ME A THANK YOU NOTE.

I think it is a good idea to send a brief thank you email after your audition. I don't need anything fancy, just a short note. Something like:

> Hello (Name of person you auditioned for. Make sure you spell it correctly.),
>
> Thanks so much for the audition yesterday. I really enjoyed meeting you. I am very interested in working with you, so please let me know if you need to see anything else from me.
>
> I look forward to talking with you more.
>
> All the best,
Your name
Your email address
Your cell number

I recommend you attach a PDF of your picture and resume to the email. I will talk more about pictures and resumes later in the book.

It's always nice to get a brief thank you note, and it will make me think nice things about you. However, it is also a good strategic move.

When I get back to my office after a few days of auditions, I go through my notes and the pictures and resumes and decide who is getting a callback. If I've just received a thank you email from you, my brain is going to spend a little more time with you than with others, and the more positive time I spend with you the more likely you are to get a callback.

However, you need to read the (virtual) room. I don't need a long email, and I don't need multiple emails. A brief thank you is just enough to remind me to spend a little more time with your file before making a final decision.

CHECK YOUR EMAIL AT LEAST ONCE A DAY.

Most if not all of our communication is going to be by email. If I want to see more of your work, I will email you. If I want to accept you to my school, I will email you. If I want to offer you a job, I will email you.

I understand that many of you communicate through texts and social media, and that is fine. However, as of right now, we are not making offers via text or social media. We use email, so please check your email at least once a day.

And please respond to my email within 36 hours. You don't have to give me an answer in 36 hours, I just need to know that you received the email.

If you can give me an answer in 36 hours, that is great, but if you need more time, send me an email that says something like this:

> Hello (Name of person who sent you the email. Be sure to spell the name correctly.),
>
> Thanks so much for the email. I am so happy that you are interested in me. I will be sure to have an answer for you before the deadline. Please let me know if you need more information from me.
>
> I look forward to talking with you more.
>
> All the best,
Your name
Your email address
Your cell number

Please make sure to give me an answer by the deadline. Don't make me chase after you.

DON'T GHOST ME.

Years ago I accepted a young woman into the conservatory. Let's call her Sally. Sally accepted her spot, and we started the registration process. We were about a month away from the first day of the Conservatory, and I tried to contact her for some last minute information. She didn't respond. I emailed her again, no response. Over the next ten days I called her, left messages, but no response. I finally left her one more message letting her know that if I didn't hear from her in 48 hours, I would have to give her spot to an alternate. I never heard from her.

Five years later I am in LA holding auditions for PCPA's professional season. I'm casting *Mamma Mia*, and I am looking for someone to play Sophie. I open the door to let the next actor in, and there stands Sally. She had no idea I was the casting director for PCPA's professional company.

She looked shocked when she saw me. She laughed awkwardly and walked in the room. I greeted her kindly, and I told her it was great to see her again. She responded, "Yeah, that was pretty crazy." I told her that I was glad to know that she was ok, and she did her audition and left.

I didn't hire her.

She was good, and she could have been in the running for the role, but my previous experience with her led me to believe that she was a flake and that she lacked integrity. I have so many wonderful actors from which to choose. I don't need to reward someone who lacks integrity.

Let me be clear, my decision not to hire her had nothing to do with her changing her mind and deciding not to come to the conservatory. I completely understand that other opportunities present themselves that cause one to change one's mind. I've hired actors for the professional company who have changed their minds about attending the conservatory. The difference between those actors and Sally is that they communicated with me. They let me know that circumstances had changed, and they would no longer be able to attend. I get emails like that a few times a year as a recruiter and as a casting director. I'm always sad to lose someone, but I always respond that I wish them all the best and that I look forward to the next time our paths cross. And I mean that sincerely. If you communicate with me, if you stand in the center of your integrity, I will look for ways we can work together in the future.

Please don't be afraid to say no. I would much rather have you turn down my offer than disappear. If you tell me no, I can then wish you well and move on. If you just don't respond, I then wonder if you got my email. I worry it went to your spam folder. I spend a lot of time and energy chasing after you to get a response.

In my world, "No" is good. I like "Yes" better, but if you tell me "No", I can then check you off my list and move on to the next person. Don't be afraid to say "No."

WRITE LEGIBLY WHENEVER YOU WRITE YOUR EMAIL ADDRESS AND CELL NUMBER.

You would be amazed by the number of people who do not get to come to my school or work at my theatre because I could not decipher their email address or cell phone number. Some of the most talented people may not even get to audition because their handwriting is so bad.

I often visit schools or festivals and meet young actors who want more information about my school and/or theatre. They put their email address on a list for more information, but they never get it because I could not read their handwriting. I've seen great work at festivals by young actors looking for a place to train, and I've asked those young actors to leave their name and contact information with my assistant, but I never get to follow up with those young actors because they didn't take the time to make sure I can read their writing.

Every time you write your email address or cell number on a piece of paper, take the time to write it like your future depends on it.

EMPTY YOUR VOICEMAIL, SO I CAN LEAVE YOU A MESSAGE.

I know texting is the preferred method of communication, but please make sure I can leave you a message on your voicemail. It is quite common for me to encounter a full voicemail when trying to leave an important message.

I understand that you like to save special messages, but make sure there is enough room for decision makers to leave you a message.

FILL OUT FORMS WHEN ASKED.

I spend quite a bit of time every year reminding young actors to fill out online forms that I've sent them. I will like you so much more if you fill out the form right when I send it to you.

Chances are it is a short online form that will take less than 15 minutes to fill out. Just follow the link and fill it out right when you get the email. If you wait to fill it out, it is common for it to be forgotten—buried under many less important emails.

Honestly, if I have to contact you to remind you to fill out your forms, I like you a little less. Every year I take note of the people who finish their online paperwork first, and I take note of those who make me remind them again and again.

I worry that some young actors think that being an actor means you get to be spacey, flakey, and unreliable. I worry that young actors think that makes them a free spirited non-conforming artist. It doesn't. It makes people think you are spacey, flakey, and unreliable. I have so many talented actors to choose from. I just don't have the time or the patience to deal with unreliable people.

Professional actors are some of the smartest people I know. They are extremely reliable, and they can multi-task better than just about anyone.

Let's change the perception of actors. Let's show the world that we are some of the most kind, intelligent, open, brave, giving, accepting, fascinating, and reliable neighbors one could ever hope for.

Jerik Fernandez, Myles Romo, Johnny Davison, Tyler Matthew Campbell, Quincy Van Steenberge

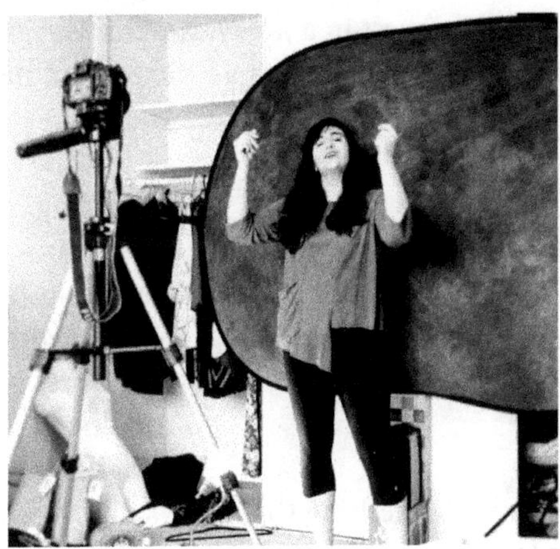

Maya Sherer

VIDEO AUDITIONS

Most, if not all, schools and training programs accept video auditions. In fact, many schools are now asking for videos first as a way to pre-screen those interested in their program. About half of the students I accept, start the process with a video audition. I recommend to students who live out of state and want to audition for my school to send a video audition for the first round and then fly in if they receive a callback.

Nothing compares to being in the room when auditioning. I think it is very important to be in the room at least once during the audition process. We want the opportunity to figure out if we want to spend two to four years together. However, video and Skype auditions are not just the future, they are becoming the norm.

I would not be surprised if in the next ten years video auditions replace my audition tour. I bet that in the not too distant future, I will no longer travel from city to city to see auditions. I will watch the first round of auditions on my iPad or on my computer in my office, and then I will invite those I am interested in to travel to us for a day of callbacks.

Video and Skype auditions are not hard. In fact, your generation is so used to being filmed, I think this will be easy for you.

You do not need to invest in a fancy camera. The camera on your smart phone is very good. It's better than the camera that filmed my wedding.

Willow Orthwein

Set the camera on something, so that it is still during your audition. You don't want it to be shaky. ***Get the camera on the same level as your face.*** You do not want it to shoot up at you. Put it on a shelf or on a stack of books, something that allows it to shoot straight at you on the same level as your face.

Make sure you turn the phone sideways so you are filming in landscape or horizontal mode. I can't see you as well in vertical mode. In horizontal mode, you fill the whole screen when I watch.

Make sure that you are closer to the camera than the source of your accompaniment. If you have a live piano player, make sure you are closer to the camera than the piano. If you are using recorded music, make sure you are closer to the camera than the speaker. You do not want your accompaniment to be louder than you.

I recommend you use recorded accompaniment when shooting a video audition. Recorded accompaniment allows you to take your time. If you are paying an accompanist, you may feel rushed. You can have a friend in the room with you to start and stop the accompaniment, or you can do it yourself.

Be aware of what is behind you. Hopefully you can film in your theatre space at your school or at your community theatre, however, if you are filming in your home or in your room, find a blank wall or hang a blanket or *ironed* sheet behind you. You do not want me to be distracted by your background. Find or create a plain background that compliments what you are wearing.

I once received a video audition that was filmed in front of a wall of dolls. It was not only distracting, it was creepy.

Make sure that you don't have too much light behind you—i.e., avoid filming in front of a window. If there is light behind you, you end up looking like a shadow. Make sure you are the best-lit thing in the shot.

If you are auditioning via Skype, make sure you have a strong internet connection. You do not want the video to freeze during your audition. Test it out before you Skype with the decision maker. Also, make sure the camera is level with your face. You do not want the camera to shoot up at you. Do a Skype dress rehearsal with a friend or coach.

We need to see your whole body at some point during the audition. You could film one piece from the waist up, which will allow me to get a good look at your face, film the next piece full body, so I get an idea of your body type, and the third piece can be your choice. You could introduce yourself waist up or full body, whatever works for you works for me. It's your show. I just want to get a good look at your face, and I want to see your whole body at some point during the audition.

If one of your pieces is very physical, that might be the one to shoot from further away. This will allow me to see your whole body and give you the freedom to move. If one of your pieces is more still, then zoom in to a half body shot, and let me see your face.

If you think all of your pieces work better in a half body shot, then frame your intro in a full body shot.

The goal is to make your video audition feel like you are auditioning for me live. I recommend you treat the camera the same way you would treat the decision maker behind the desk if you were auditioning in person.

- Start your audition by introducing yourself. Look right into the lens and try to connect with me.

- For your first piece, look just slightly to one side of the camera. For your second piece, look just slightly to the other side.

- Make sure you are very clear about who you are talking to. Have a brief yet obvious moment before. Fight to change your other. Make life-altering discovery, deal with something unexpected, change your tactics, and fight to win. Have a brief moment after.

- When you are finished, reconnect with the decision maker

through the lens. Say thank you, then fade to black with your contact information displayed on the screen. Some people fade to their resume picture with their contact info just below the picture.

I recommend you film your pieces separately. This will allow you to choose the best takes of each of your pieces. You can then edit them together in one clip, or you can send three different well-labeled links.

Make sure you follow the guidelines for video auditions outlined by the school. They may ask you to send all of your pieces in one long shot without any cutting, or they may ask for several different links. If they ask for something specific, do it. If they don't, then make your own show. Your best bet is to film something you would want to see if you were watching hundreds of video auditions. No caution!

I think the hardest thing about video auditions is picking your best take. You will never be fully satisfied with your work. There will always be something you would like to do again, and you will drive yourself crazy trying to get the perfect take. I suggest you film each of your pieces three times and then have someone you trust pick your best take. I recommend you ask someone who knows the theatre business to pick your best take—someone like your teacher, a local theatre director, or a sophisticated alumni. Your parents are awesome, but they may not know the industry well enough to pick the piece that shows you off the best.

I recommend you send your video link using YouTube (on the ***unlisted*** setting) or Vimeo. You want it to be as easy as possible for the decision maker to see your video. If the school outlines how they want you to submit the video, follow the instructions closely. If they do not have clear instructions, then make it as easy as possible. ***Do not make me subscribe to your YouTube channel.*** If I need a password to see the video, make sure it is very clear and easy for me to make it work.

The best links are the ones I can click on and the video immediately starts. I like YouTube on the unlisted setting. This means anyone who has the link can watch the video. All they need to do is click on the link, and YouTube immediately starts playing the video. It is still an exclusive video. Only those with the link can watch it, but it is easy. One click and I am watching your show.

You will want to include the links to your videos in a short professional email. Here is a sample:

> November 16th, 2018
>
> Hello,
>
> My name is Joel Kneedler, and I am very interested in your two year Acting Conservatory. My friend Teresa Hildebridle is currently a student, and she speaks very highly of the training you offer.
>
> Below are links to three audition pieces. I've also attached my picture and resume. Please let me know if you would like anything else from me.
>
> Contemporary- Ken from *Silent Night Holy $#*+*: https://www.youtube.com/watch?v=3xxaNP-mz0NE&feature=youtu.be
>
> Classical- Clarence from *Richard III:* https://www.youtube.com/watch?v=3zzaNPmz0NE&feature=youtu.be
>
> Song- "I'm a Great Big Baby" from *Eubie:* https://www.youtube.com/watch?v=3yyaNPmz0NE&feature=youtu.be
>
> I look forward to talking with you more.
>
> All the best,
> Joel
>
> Joel Kneedler
> Email address
> Phone number

I like having separate links for each of your pieces. That way if I want to watch your song again, I don't need to fast forward through your monologues. However, you should follow the instructions outlined by the school. If they want one link for all three of your pieces, then you could label it like this:

> Joel Kneedler's Conservatory audition
> https://www.youtube.com/watch?v=3zzaNP-mz0NE&feature=youtu.be

If you have separate links, start each link by connecting with the decision maker through the lens, say your name and the title of the piece, then fade or transition to the piece. Let me see your brief yet obvious moment before. If you have one link, start by connecting with the decision maker through the lens, introduce all three of your pieces, then fade to your first piece, cut or fade to your second piece, then cut or fade to your third piece. You can also shoot it all in one take.

The secret to a video audition is to treat the camera as if it is the decision maker. Act just like you would if you were walking into a studio, and I was sitting behind the table. Talk to the camera as if it were me; let me see the authentic you.

It's opening night, and I am lucky, because I have a video of your show. Let me see you transform, let me see you get messy and take risks, let me see you fight to change your other, let me see you fight to win.

In a video, you only get one shot. I can't give you direction and ask you to do it again. So bring it. Send me links to you at your best. No caution!

Maya Sherer

Brittany Law

CALLBACKS

The purpose of this book is to help you create an audition that will get you called back. I could write another book just on callbacks, but for now, here are a few tips to give you an advantage.

Most reputable training programs have some sort of callback process. Many have extensive callbacks that last the whole day.

At UCLA you may start with a question and answer period, then go to one room and do your monologues, another room to sing, another room to dance, and then end with an interview.

If you are called back to Julliard, you will take several classes over the course of a few days. They watch you participate as if you've already been accepted. They lead discussions and classes, and they watch how you thrive in the Julliard environment.

I see about 500 actors either by video or during my audition tour. I call back 65, and we accept 30.

Our callback process starts at 9:00 a.m. and ends around 9:30 p.m. The day starts with a group warm-up. We then have each actor show the entire faculty one of their audition pieces from their first audition. Then we have a question and answer session where the students can ask current students questions. The faculty is not present during this, so the current students feel free to speak freely. We then take a lunch break.

After lunch the students are invited to see a performance of our current mainstage production. Then there is a dinner break. After dinner, we put the students into four groups, and each group goes through four 45 minute workshops. They participate in an acting workshop, a singing workshop, a movement/dance workshop, and a text/Shakespeare workshop. Each workshop is lead by different faculty members, and other faculty members stand around with clipboards and watch. After the workshops, we regroup for a quick goodbye.

You should assume that you are being watched at all times. I even have current students disguised as called back actors, so I can hear what goes on when I am not in the room. This should not concern you. Just be the awesome person you are.

The best advice I can give is lean forward and let us see you. We are watching a lot of people, and we have to make decisions quickly. Participate all the time. Even when you are listening, lean forward. Don't allow yourself to become just an observer. Support your fellow actors. Root for them, and make sure you are taking your opportunities to be seen.

Remember, poised is poisonous. Don't hide behind being polite. You need to be comfortable putting yourself in a position to be seen. You also want your fellow actors to be seen. It's almost as if you are saying, "Look at me, and also look at her." When in doubt, remember the golden rule: treat others the way you would want to be treated.

If we call you back, the assumption is that you have the skill set to attend our school. We now want to figure out if you are the type of person we want to spend two years with, if you are hungry for everything we offer, and if you will work well with the faculty and your fellow students. We are looking to put together a group of collaborative actors who work well together. We want actors who will seize every opportunity we offer and support their fellow actors.

Any callback will be what you make of it, so lean forward and bring your authentic self to the process. Read the energy of the room. Be playful yet sophisticated. Contribute to the conversation and actively listen to others. Be aware of what is going on around you, trust your instincts, be bold, take up space, and let me say it again: READ

THE ENERGY OF THE ROOM.

It's rare that you will be able to please everyone, so let's not focus on that. Instead, focus on being the actor you would want to have in your program. Bring your confident and nurturing self, bring your skills, bring your kindness, bring your bravery. No caution!

INTERVIEW

Most reputable schools will have some sort of interview process. It may be at your initial audition or it may be during the callbacks. You may not even know it's happening, but if a decision maker is asking you questions, you can assume it is an interview.

The reason for an interview is to get to know you. We want to see how well you think on your feet. Will you let us see the authentic you? Are you comfortable expressing your thoughts to an authority figure?

It's hard to fully prepare for an interview, but you can practice. Here are a couple of interview tips:

- Lean forward during the interview. Maybe even put your hands on the table.
- Look the interviewer in the eyes, and try to connect.
- Hear the question and then elaborate when answering.
- Read the energy coming from the person behind the table.
- Be the host of the event, and put them at ease.

You must be ready to answer, ***"Why do you want to be a part of this program/school?"*** Here are some things one might look for in a program. These are not meant to be memorized. Hopefully, they will get you thinking about what you are looking for in a program:

- I am looking for a program that sees our training as a journey. A program where I can focus on staying in the moment, and take advantage of every opportunity that presents itself.
- I want to be ready to work professionally when I graduate.

I may decide to go on to grad school, but I want to feel ready to work professionally after graduation.

• I know a program's success relies heavily on how much I am willing to invest of myself. I want strong mentors who are excited by a student who wants to take advantage of every opportunity he, she, or they can and embrace any obstacle that is put in their way.

• I want to be part of a program that is producing the top students in the country. Students who work and can shape the future of the American theatre.

You need to be able to answer, ***"Why did you pick this audition piece?"*** "Because my teacher gave it to me" is NOT a good answer What is it about the character that attracted you?

- Is the character in a situation that is familiar to you?
- Did it challenge you in some way?
- Can you relate it to something in your life?
- Is the character of your generation or your age and fun for you to relate to?
- Does the character's passion speak to you?
- Do the character's flaws interest you or make you laugh?
- Maybe the character is very different from you, and it is exciting to explore someone so different.

They are going to ask you if you have any questions for them. ***You should definitely ask questions.*** It shows you are interested, engaged, curious, prepared, and that you are weighing your options. You could ask two questions but no more than three.

Possible Questions (if you have your own that's great):
Do you have a cut system?
If yes, do you have mandatory cuts?

> **Note:** A cut system is a system where at the end of the year or semester some students get cut from the program. Mandatory cuts are where a school starts with 30 students, but have already decided they will only graduate 15. They must cut 15 students before the final year.

> **Rant:** Personally, I don't like cut systems. I think a program should have very high standards, and if an actor does not meet those standards, they should not be asked back for the next semester. However, I think cut systems breed a cautious environment. To be an actor you must feel comfortable taking risks. You must risk failing. If you are constantly worried about being cut, you will not risk failing. You will just focus on doing what you need to do to stay ahead of your classmates. My wonderful friend and PCPA graduate Scott Fuss summed it up so well by saying, "I do not want my success based on someone else's failure."

Do first year students have opportunities to perform on the main stage, or do they focus on work in the classroom and studio?

What's great about this question is you can respond positively to whatever the answer is.

Are your professors/faculty still working as professional actors and directors?

> **Note:** I think it is important to be taught by people who actually do this instead of being taught by people who used to do this. The industry changes. I want you to be ready to enter today's market, not the market of 10 years ago.

You should also be prepared to answer random questions. Questions you will never be able to predict. They want to see you think on your feet. When answering these types of questions, try to venture away from the theatre. Talk about other aspects of your life. Talk about your family, traveling, other academic subjects that interest you—let me see your passions.

Questions like:

- What is your greatest strength?
- What is your biggest weakness?
- What is your biggest success in life so far?
- What is your biggest failure so far, and what did you learn from it?
- Where do you see yourself in five years? In ten years?
- What book have you read recently that had a profound effect on you, and how did it affect you?
- If you could go back in history and change one thing before 1900 what would it be and why?
- If you could have dinner with one historical figure who would it be and why?

There are no right or wrong answers. Don't overthink, just trust your gut. Hear the question, connect with the person behind the table, and elaborate. We want you to do most of the talking. In fact, I like it when the energy shifts, and it feels like you are interviewing me. The best interviews are the ones that become conversations. No caution!

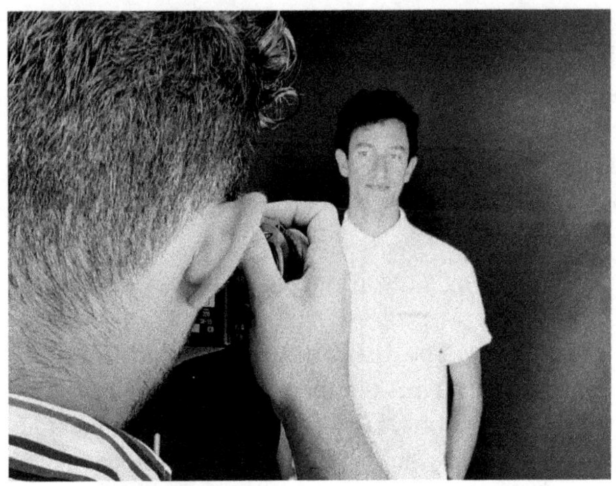

Christian Zumbado and Tiago Santos

PICTURE AND RESUME

Your picture and resume are often the first thing I receive from you. They are your first impression. They are also what we use to remember you after the audition tour. Your picture and resume are what we spread out on the floor when we are narrowing it down from 500 to 65. Your picture and resume are what I show the faculty when we are selecting 30 from 65. Take the time to make sure they represent you well.

PICTURES:

Most reputable programs will ask for a headshot.

It is hard to describe how to take a good resume picture or "headshot" in a book. The best advice I can give is to look at professional headshots online and take note of what you like and what is currently trending.

I think the best headshot photographer in the country is Dirty Sugar. They are VERY expensive, and I do not think you need to spend anywhere near that much money for your college audition picture. However, you can get an idea of what you like by visiting their website. Print or save your favorites. Show them to your photographer. This will get everyone on the same page. Here is a link to some Dirty Sugar headshots.: https://dirtysugar.smugmug.com/Portfolio/Website-Marketing/Current-Website- Galleries/Website-Portfolio-Color/

> **Note:** I strongly recommend you do not search "headshots" or "professional headshots" on the internet. You will be directed to some very disturbing images. I found this out the hard way. When searching for professional headshots, make sure to include the words "actor" and "photographer". You should be safe if you search "professional actor headshot photographers".

A couple of things to keep in mind:

Your photo should be in color. It should be 8 inches by 10 inches. It can be a vertical shot or a horizontal shot. Do not use a glossy finish. The picture should be primarily your shoulders and head, that is why it is called a headshot. If you want to show more of your body, that is fine, but your face should be the most important part of the picture. Your resume should be stapled to the back of the picture. Your resume will be printed on 8 1/2 by 11 inch paper, so you will need to cut your resume to fit nicely on the back of your picture.

Mitchell Lam Hau Photo Credit - Zumbado Photography

A photo shoot can be a bit awkward at first. It will probably take you about 50 frames to get warmed up and comfortable. Bring two to three different outfits, and wear your least favorite outfit first.

The most important part of the picture is your eyes. Your eyes show us who you are. Your eyes are more revealing if they are engaged, so play an intention during the photo shoot. Everything in life is better with an intention. Don't allow your eyes to glaze over. Do not hold a pose too long, because your eyes will glaze over. Only hold a pose for three or four clicks of the camera. Look into the lens (click, click, click, click) look away, look back into the lens, (click, click, click) look away, repeat.

Look directly into the lens. Try to look through the lens. Try to connect with the person in the lens. Play an intention. I suggest you play, "I want to share my secret." Keep thinking, "I have a secret, do you want to know it?" Make sure it is a positive, fun secret. It could even be slightly ridiculous. Something like, "I have peanut butter in my belly button." Something fun that will make you smile. Make sure that your other inside the lens of the camera is someone you trust and want to share your secret with.

Caroline Whelehan.
Photo Credit - Zumbado Photography

If you've got a super fun secret, then I will see something in your eyes that draws me in and makes me want to know more. If you want to share it with me, then I will think you trust me, and both of us will feel at ease.

Ladies, don't wear too much make-up. You want to have a fresh look, but you don't want to look too made up. This is not a glamour shot. You need to look like your headshot when you arrive at the audition.

Guys, I suggest you wear a little bit of tinted moisturizer that matches the color of your skin. You want to look healthy, but not orange. We've all seen orange people who look ridiculous. Go to a make-up counter, and get the advice of a professional. Tell the person behind the counter that you are getting close-up pictures taken, and you need tinted moisturizer that matches your skin.

Do your research, so you can show your photographer what you are hoping for, get good sleep the night before, and have fun. You should feel good every time you look at your picture.

RESUMES:

Most reputable programs will ask you to provide a resume. Your resume should be well laid out. Use the tab button to make sure all of your columns and spacing line up. You want it to look sharp, clean, easy to read, and professional. It should only be one page because it needs to fit on the back of your picture. Pick the credits and training that highlight you the most.

Let your name be big at the top. Follow that with your height and voice type. Some people include their weight, but that is not necessary. Only include your weight if you think it makes you unique: i.e., I am 6 foot 6 inches, and I include my weight, 255 lbs, because it advertises that I am a big guy.

You should also have your contact information at the top and easy to find. I need your email address and your cell phone number. This might be the most important part of your resume. Be sure there is contact information. You would be amazed by how many resumes I get from students who forget to include their contact information.

Do not include your home address on your resume. We do not need to send you anything via snail mail, and resumes often end up in the trash. You do not want random people to find a picture of you with your address in the trash.

Next, list your most impressive credits. They do not need to be in chronological order. Put your most impressive credits first. Include the title, the character you played, and where you performed the play. You can also include who directed the play, but that is not necessary. Include the name if you think it is someone we might know.

I also would like to see a section devoted to your training. List schools you have attended that included theatre training—i.e. your high school if you took drama classes, after school community theatre classes, summer training programs like Northwestern's Cherubs, Walnut Hill, Interlochen, Camp Bravo, etc. List the classes you've taken and who taught them. List any special masterclasses you've been a part of. Did someone special lead a workshop at your school? Did you take a masterclass with someone cool at the Thespian Festival? Have you taken private voice lessons? How many years of dance classes have you taken?

At the bottom of your resume include some special skills. Do you juggle? Experience with stage combat? Proficient with dialects? Eat fire? Improv? Play sports? SCUBA Dive? Whatever you put on your resume, make sure you can actually do it. Chances are someone will ask.

The goal of your resume should be to give an easy-to-read overview of your experience and training. It is also a great way to get the names of people who know and love your work into the discussion. If I see someone I know on your resume, chances are I will call them and ask them about you. A good recommendation from someone I trust goes a long way when I am trying to narrow it down from 500 to 65 and then from 65 to 30.

Here is a sample resume.

Taylor Hart

HEIGHT: 5' 6" | 805.456.7891
VOICE: Soprano/Mezzo, Belter(C6-E3) | thart@gmail.com

THEATRE

The Fantasticks	Luisa	SLO Rep/David Foster
Addams Family	Ensemble/(US) Wednesday	PCPA/Erik Stein
Gentleman's Guide	Ensemble/(US) Phoebe	PCPA/Brad Carroll
Theory of Relativity	Mira	PCPA Rep/Peter Hadres
Hunchback of Notre Dame	Ensemble/(US) Gargoyle	PCPA/Brad Carroll
Peter Pan	Ensemble	PCPA/Mark Booher
Guys and Dolls	Sarah Brown	PCT/Charles Davidson
Sister Act	Mary Robert	STAC/Ray Ashton
Dog Sees God	CB's Sister	PCPA Project

TRAINING

Pacific Conservatory Theatre Professional Actor Training Program
- Acting - Roger DeLaurier, Peter Hadres, George Walker, Polly Firestone-Walker
- Shakespeare - Andrew Philpot, Don Stewart
- Ballet - Valerie Kline
- Musical Theatre Dance - Lindy Booher
- Movement - Katie Fuchs-Wackowski
- Singing Techniques - Brad Carroll, Paul Marszalkowski
- Voice, Speech, and Dialect - Kitty Balay, Yusef Seevers
- Combat - Peter Hadres

Choral Vocal Training - 10 years
Dance - Ballet (8 yrs), Jazz (8 yrs), Hip Hop (3 yrs), Tap (4 yrs), En Pointe (5 yrs)

WORKSHOPS

Vocal - Laura Bell Bundy, Lee Lessack, Leslie Noel, Mary Jo DuPrey
Stage Combat - Orion Barnes
Acting - Faith Prince
Suzuki/ Viewpoints Master Course - Stephanie Courtney

SPECIAL SKILLS

-Head stand, Tap (intermediate), Rattan work, Human Kazoo, Can look two ways at once, Juggling, Painting

This is the format LA agents use for their theatre clients. I suggest you use this format. I strongly recommend that when you send your resume as an attachment in an email, you send it as a PDF. If you send it as a PDF, you know that the person viewing your resume sees exactly what you see. If you send it in other formats, the spacing can get all wonky.

Your resume is part of your first impression. Take the time to make it look well put together. Line up the columns, make sure the spacing looks good. Make it look well planned, clear, and easy to read. Make sure it is worthy of you.

> **Advice:** Often people ask what advice I can give students interested in being competitive for the top schools in the country. One of the first things I look for on a resume is dance training. Actors who are comfortable in their own skin are desirable. And young actors often struggle with living in their skin. Actors with dance training are often ready for more sophisticated training. Obviously, a skilled dancer is very useful when casting musicals. If you are a guy and you dance well, chances are you will have your pick of training programs. However, you do not need to be a stellar dancer to reap the benefits of dance training. A lot of young actors exist from their chest up. Dance training will help you live in your whole body. It will help you take up space in a room full of big personalities. It will teach you to use your whole body in a tactical way. I don't care how old you are, I don't care what you look like. If you want to do this for a living, get into a dance class. Learn how your body moves. Learn what it is to radiate from every pore in your body.

Madison Davis

EPILOGUE

MY PHILOSOPHY:

Many say that this is a competitive business, but that is not how I look at it. So much is subjective, so much is out of your control. How can you compete if there are no rules? So instead of competition, I think about opportunity.

The opportunities go to those who show up. The roles go to those who show up. Decisions are made by those who show up. Life is truly lived by those who show up. Don't sit back and comment on life, show up and engage. Someone smarter than me once said that luck is when opportunity meets preparation. You need to embrace every opportunity.

If you show up, you will leave a better person no matter what happens. There is so much to learn just by being in the room with others. Take note of how many people I mentioned in this book.

Everything I know came from collaboration. I am a better actor because I was in the room with Derrick Weeden. I am a better director because I assisted Paul Barnes. I am a better teacher because I sat behind the table with Brad Carroll. I am a better mentor because Sandra Dinse took the time to listen to me. I am a better leader because Mark Booher trusted my opinion. And I am a better man because I married Jacqueline Hildebrand.

Don't compete with others. Lift others up. My wonderful friend and mentor Neal LaVine told me that actors are the last of the great explorers. We explore what it is to be human. Let's explore together. Your success is not based on someone else's failure. We must collaborate and celebrate, communicate and commiserate, congratulate and participate, appreciate, illuminate, integrate, vindicate, be passionate, all so that we can create.

FINAL THOUGHTS:

My hope is that this book gives you confidence. Those of us behind the table are rooting for you. We want you to be exactly what we are looking for. The vast majority of the decision makers you encounter will be kind and helpful. They will welcome you and guide you the moment you walk into the audition room. However, I want to be sure you know exactly what to do if the person behind the table never says a word.

I want you to stand in the hallway excited to show me your opening night performance, and hopefully the steps I've outlined will help you show me your passion, your preparation, and your potential with absolutely no caution.

Yet it is important for you to remember that there are no black and white rules. Auditioning exists in a world of grey. What one person likes, another may find monotonous. What I think is hysterical another may find absurd. So what! Painters don't paint pictures to please people. They paint the picture they want to paint, then they invite people to see it, and they hope it affects them in a positive way.

Why should actors be any different? We create shows that mean something to us. We put our hearts and souls into these shows, and we invite people to come see what we have created. We hope that those that see what we create respond positively, but that is not why we do it. We do it, because life is meant to be shared. We do it to connect. We do it to ask the questions that we don't yet have the answers to and to question our assumptions. We do it because it is thrilling, and we do it because we have to.

And when we do it, we must do it well. We must do it with passion, we must do it with skill, we must do it with preparation, and we must do it with no caution.

That would have been a great way to end the book. Why am I still writing? The last two words were the title. Pretty clever, right? But I'm not quite finished yet. I have one more quick story.

My high school drama teacher, Leslie Hinshaw, asked me a question when I was 16 that changed my life. He asked me, "Erik, when you go to a party and someone asks you to bring the ice cream, what flavor do you bring?" He said, you could bring vanilla. Everybody likes vanilla. Everybody will probably have some of the vanilla, but nobody will remember the vanilla. The vanilla will be quickly forgotten. But what if you bring Chunky Monkey? Banana ice cream, with chunks of dark chocolate and walnuts. Some people are not going to like that ice cream, some people may even be angry that you brought it. Others will love the ice cream. Some may say it is the best ice cream they have ever had. It is hard to predict who will like it and who won't, but you can bet people will remember the ice cream. They may even still be talking about the ice cream the next day. Some may even invite you to the next party just because they liked your Chunky Monkey.

All you have to do is prepare, show me your potential, and share your passion. The authentic you is Chunky Monkey. If you try to be something you think I want, well, that's vanilla. You are worthy of greatness. Trust me when I say, "You are enough." Nobody does you better than you.

"Anything you do
let it come from you
then it will be new.
Give us more to see..."

Sunday in the Park with George by Stephen Sondheim

Ella Ruth Francis, Natalia Womack, Myles Romo, Jerik Fernandez, Vintre Scott, Brandon Jones Mooney, Johnny Davison, and Erin Sarmiento

SPECIAL THANKS

Jacqueline Hildebrand
Chrissy Collins
Aleah Van Woert
Marisa Dinsmoor
Kathryn Blanche
Tamara Stein
Karin Hendricks
Jonathan Dorf
Paul Metchik
Charlotte Baldiviez
Roger DeLaurier
Kitty Balay
Christian Zumbado
Carley Herlihy
My Students
My Colleagues
My Mentors
And my mom, Ann Stein

Photo Credit - Lucas Blair Photography

ABOUT THE AUTHOR

Erik Stein is the Casting Director for PCPA Pacific Conservatory Theatre and the Recruitment Coordinator for Pacific Conservatory Theatre's Professional Actor Training Program. On Broadway, Erik performed with Roddy McDowall, Hal Linden, Jim Dale, and Frank Langella. He appeared as the Ghost of Christmas Present opposite Tim Curry in the Broadway production of *A Christmas Carol* directed by Susan Stroman. Off-Broadway, Erik created the role of Stephens in Manhattan Theatre Club's production of *Captains Courageous* starring Treat Williams and Norm Lewis. Erik is a founding member of The Alaska Shakespeare Festival and The California Cabaret Theatre. He has had the fortune to work across the country with more than 30 Regional Theaters including several award-winning theaters such as The York Theatre Company, Goodspeed Opera House, The Utah Shakespeare Festival, Pioneer Theatre Company, North Shore Music Theatre, Geva Theatre, Theatre Under the Stars, and PCPA. Erik teaches Audition Techniques and the Business of Being an Actor, he has directed for several training programs and regional theaters, and he has lead Audition and Acting the Song workshops all over the country. As a playwright, Erik has written a few plays including *Under the Boardwalk, Ho, Oh, No! A Christmas Show!, Mouth Pictures,* and *The Key*. Erik lives with his beautiful wife Jax and their two wonderful cats on the Central Coast of California. You can reach Erik at NoCautiontheBook@gmail.com.

Printed in the USA
CPSIA information can be obtained
at www.ICGtesting.com
LVHW011208280723
753395LV00014B/844

9 780578 549736